BIBLE
WISDOM
FOR Mothers

COMPILED BY GARY WILDE
AND CAROL WILDE

Christian
Parenting
BOOKS

Christian Parenting Books is an imprint of Chariot Family Publishing, a division of David C. Cook Publishing Co., Elgin, Illinois 60120 David C. Cook Publishing Co., Weston, Ontario Nova Distribution Ltd., Newton Abbot, England

Christian Parenting Today Magazine P.O. Box 850, Sisters, OR 97759 (800) 238-2221

BIBLE WISDOM FOR MOTHERS ©1993 by Chariot Family Publishing

Cover design by Foster Design Associates Interior Design by Glass House Graphics Compiled by Gary Wilde

First Printing, 1993   ISBN 0-78140-073-2 Printed in the United States of America 97 96 95 94   5 4 3

TABLE OF CONTENTS

What Values Are You Modeling?
- Delilah: A Woman of Deceitful Values
- Sapphira: A Woman Who Valued Money Too Highly
- Dorcas: A Woman of Good Works

God's Values to Teach Your Children
- Perseverance
- Thoughtfulness
- Happiness
- Honesty
- Compassion
- Faith

CHAPTER 8 131
'How can I handle the pain I feel over the loss of a child?'

Facing the Tragedy
- A Woman Suffering Great Loss
- A Mother Grieving in the Wrong Way
- Husbands Feeling the Pain, Too

God Comforts Us in Our Loss
- He Never Forsakes Us
- He Provides the Reward of Heaven
- He Brings an End to Death and Grief Forever

Helping Your Kids Know the Awesome God
- He Is All-Powerful
- He Is All-Knowing and Wise
- He Is Patient
- He Is Merciful
- He is Faithful
- He Seeks Faithful Worshipers

Teaching Your Kids Who Jesus Is
- He Was God Incarnate
- He Claimed to Be Deity
- He Bore Our Sins

CHAPTER 1

'Where can I turn for the courage and energy I need to be a good mom?'

I never would have thought 'courage' would be a word that came to mind when I first started thinking about becoming a mother years ago," said Jenny. "But now I can see that's just what it takes to be a good mom—little acts of bravery everyday, all day long, just to keep keeping on.

"Probably the most daunting challenge is to keep my cool when everything around me gets so hectic. That's when I feel like I'm trying to balance everything

11

on my own shoulders: job, home, community and church obligations. Yes, I suppose I would like to qualify for a medal of honor. Being a good mother is that important to me."

FOR MEMORY:

Though an army besiege me, my heart will not fear; though war break out against me, even then will I be confident.

Psalm 27:3

FOR SILENT REFLECTION:

• *In what specific ways have I noticed myself acting courageously in my family lately?*

• *Has my courage failed me in any ways recently?*

• *Where do I turn when I feel my energy flagging?*

• *If I could speak directly to Jesus right now, in person, what one thing would I ask Him for—something that would make me a better mom?*

When You Become Overwhelmed with Your Parenting Responsibilities . . .

Feeling Weak and Worn Out?

Be merciful to me, LORD, for I am faint; O LORD, heal me, for my bones are in agony.

Psalm 6:2

I have seen something else under the sun:
The race is not to the swift
or the battle to the strong,
nor does food come to the wise
or wealth to the brilliant
or favor to the learned;
 but time and chance happen to them all.
Moreover, no man knows when his hour will come:
As fish are caught in a cruel net,
or birds are taken in a snare,
so men are trapped by evil times
that fall unexpectedly upon them.

Ecclesiastes 9:11, 12

That is why, for Christ's sake, I delight in weaknesses, in insults, in hardships, in persecutions, in difficulties. For when I am weak, then I am strong.

2 Corinthians 12:10

But we have this treasure in jars of clay to show that

13

this all-surpassing power is from God and not from us. We are hard pressed on every side, but not crushed; perplexed, but not in despair; persecuted, but not abandoned; struck down, but not destroyed. We always carry around in our body the death of Jesus, so that the life of Jesus may also be revealed in our body. For we who are alive are always being given over to death for Jesus' sake, so that his life may be revealed in our mortal body.

II Corinthians 4:7-11

I lift up my eyes to the hills—
where does my help come from?
My help comes from the LORD,
the Maker of heaven and earth.
He will not let your foot slip—
he who watches over you will not slumber;
indeed, he who watches over Israel
will neither slumber nor sleep.
The LORD watches over you—
the LORD is your shade at your right hand;
the sun will not harm you by day,
nor the moon by night.
The LORD will keep you from all harm—
he will watch over your life;
the LORD will watch over your coming
and going both now and forevermore.

Psalm 121:1-8

Feeling Uncertain of Your Abilities?

Be strong and courageous. Do not be afraid or terrified because of them, for the LORD your God goes with you; he will never leave you nor forsake you.

Deuteronomy 31:6

Have I not commanded you? Be strong and courageous. Do not be terrified; do not be discouraged, for the LORD your God will be with you wherever you go.

Joshua 1:9

Therefore we will not fear, though the earth give way and the mountains fall into the heart of the sea.

Psalm 46:2

Whoever listens to me will live in safety and be at ease, without fear of harm.

Proverbs 1:33

Indeed, the very hairs of your head are all numbered. Don't be afraid; you are worth more than many sparrows.

Luke 12:7

Do not be afraid, little flock, for your Father has been pleased to give you the kingdom.

Luke 12:32

15

For God did not give us a spirit of timidity, but a spirit of power, of love and of self-discipline.

II Timothy 1:7

There is no fear in love. But perfect love drives out fear, because fear has to do with punishment. The man who fears is not made perfect in love.

I John 4:18

Feeling Worried?

I tell you, do not worry about your life, what you will eat or drink; or about your body, what you will wear. Is not life more important than food, and the body more important than clothes? Look at the birds of the air; they do not sow or reap or store away in barns, and yet your heavenly Father feeds them. Are you not much more valuable than they? Who of you by worrying can add a single hour to his life? And why do you worry about clothes? See how the lilies of the field grow. They do not labor or spin.

Yet I tell you that not even Solomon in all his splendor was dressed like one of these. If that is how God clothes the grass of the field, which is here today and tomorrow is thrown into the fire, will he not much more clothe you, O you of little faith? So do not worry, saying, "What shall we eat?" or "What shall we drink?" or "What shall we wear?"

For the pagans run after all these things, and your heavenly Father knows that you need them. But seek first his kingdom and his righteousness, and all these things will be given to you as well. Therefore do not worry about tomorrow, for tomorrow will worry about itself. Each day has enough trouble of its own.

Matthew 6:25-34

Do not be anxious about anything, but in everything, by prayer and petition, with thanksgiving, present your requests to God. And the peace of God, which transcends all understanding, will guard your hearts and your minds in Christ Jesus. . . . I am not saying this because I am in need, for I have learned to be content whatever the circumstances. I know what it is to be in need, and I know what it is to have plenty. I have learned the secret of being content in any and every situation, whether well fed or hungry, whether living in plenty or in want.

Philippians 4:6-12

Feeling Ineffective?

For my days vanish like smoke;
my bones burn like glowing embers.
My heart is blighted and withered like grass;
I forget to eat my food.
Because of my loud groaning
I am reduced to skin and bones.

17

I am like a desert owl,
like an owl among the ruins. I lie awake;
I have become like a bird alone on a housetop.

Psalm 102:3-7

My disgrace is before me all day long, and my face is
covered with shame.

Psalm 44:15

Scorn has broken my heart and has left me helpless;
I looked for sympathy, but there was none, for com-
forters, but I found none.

Psalm 69:20

The LORD is close to the brokenhearted and saves
those who are crushed in spirit.

Psalm 34:18

I will exalt you, O LORD,
for you lifted me out of the depths
and did not let my enemies gloat over me.
O LORD my God, I called to you for help
and you healed me.
O LORD, you brought me up from the grave;
you spared me from going down into the pit.
Sing to the LORD, you saints of his;
praise his holy name.
For his anger lasts only a moment,

but his favor lasts a lifetime;
weeping may remain for a night,
but rejoicing comes in the morning.

Psalm 30:1-5

Cast your cares on the LORD and he will sustain you;
he will never let the righteous fall.

Psalm 55:22

He heals the brokenhearted and binds up their
wounds.

Psalm 147:3

. . . Be Inspired by Women of Heroic Spirit

Miriam: She Led in Worship

Then Miriam the prophetess, Aaron's sister, took a
tambourine in her hand, and all the women followed
her, with tambourines and dancing. Miriam sang to
them: "Sing to the LORD, for he is highly exalted.
The horse and its rider he has hurled into the sea."

Exodus 15:20,21

Deborah: She Commanded in Battle

Deborah, a prophetess, the wife of Lappidoth, was
leading Israel at that time. She held court under the
Palm of Deborah between Ramah and Bethel in the

19

hill country of Ephraim, and the Israelites came to her to have their disputes decided.

She sent for Barak son of Abinoam from Kedesh in Naphtali and said to him, "The LORD, the God of Israel, commands you: 'Go, take with you ten thousand men of Naphtali and Zebulun and lead the way to Mount Tabor. I will lure Sisera, the commander of Jabin's army, with his chariots and his troops to the Kishon River and give him into your hands.'" Barak said to her, "If you go with me, I will go; but if you don't go with me, I won't go." "Very well," Deborah said, "I will go with you. But because of the way you are going about this, the honor will not be yours, for the LORD will hand Sisera over to a woman."

So Deborah went with Barak to Kedesh, where he summoned Zebulun and Naphtali. Ten thousand men followed him, and Deborah also went with him. Now Heber the Kenite had left the other Kenites, the descendants of Hobab, Moses' brother-in-law, and pitched his tent by the great tree in Zaanannim near Kedesh. When they told Sisera that Barak son of Abinoam had gone up to Mount Tabor, Sisera gathered together his nine hundred iron chariots and all the men with him, from Harosheth Haggoyim to the Kishon River.

Then Deborah said to Barak, "Go! This is the day the LORD has given Sisera into your hands. Has not the LORD gone ahead of you?" So Barak went down

Mount Tabor, followed by ten thousand men.

Judges 4:4-14

On that day Deborah and Barak son of Abinoam sang this song: "When the princes in Israel take the lead, when the people willingly offer themselves—praise the LORD! Hear this, you kings! Listen, you rulers! I will sing to the LORD, I will sing; I will make music to the LORD, the God of Israel.

O LORD, when you went out from Seir, when you marched from the land of Edom, the earth shook, the heavens poured, the clouds poured down water. The mountains quaked before the LORD, the One of Sinai, before the LORD, the God of Israel. In the days of Shamgar son of Anath, in the days of Jael, the roads were abandoned; travelers took to winding paths. Village life in Israel ceased, ceased until I, Deborah, arose, arose a mother in Israel. When they chose new gods, war came to the city gates, and not a shield or spear was seen among forty thousand in Israel. My heart is with Israel's princes, with the willing volunteers among the people. Praise the LORD!

Judges 5:1-9

A Sick Woman: She Made Her Way to Jesus

And a woman was there who had been subject to bleeding for twelve years. She had suffered a great deal under the care of many doctors and had spent all she had, yet instead of getting better she grew worse. When she heard about Jesus, she came up behind him in the crowd and touched his cloak, because she thought, "If I just touch his clothes, I will be healed." Immediately her bleeding stopped and she felt in her body that she was freed from her suffering. At once Jesus realized that power had gone out from him. He turned around in the crowd and asked, "Who touched my clothes?"

"You see the people crowding against you," his disciples answered, "and yet you can ask, 'Who touched me?'" But Jesus kept looking around to see who had done it. Then the woman, knowing what had happened to her, came and fell at his feet and, trembling with fear, told him the whole truth.

He said to her, "Daughter, your faith has healed you. Go in peace and be freed from your suffering."

Mark 5:25-34

A Greek Woman: She Bravely Persisted

Jesus left that place and went to the vicinity of Tyre. He entered a house and did not want anyone to know it; yet he could not keep his presence secret. In fact, as soon as she heard about him, a woman whose little daughter was possessed by an evil spirit came and fell at his feet.

The woman was a Greek, born in Syrian Phoenicia. She begged Jesus to drive the demon out of her daughter. "First let the children eat all they want," he told her, "for it is not right to take the children's bread and toss it to their dogs." "Yes, Lord," she replied, "but even the dogs under the table eat the children's crumbs."

Then he told her, "For such a reply, you may go; the demon has left your daughter." She went home and found her child lying on the bed, and the demon gone.

Mark 7:24-30

Pilate's Wife: She Spoke on Behalf of Jesus

While Pilate was sitting on the judge's seat, his wife sent him this message: "Don't have anything to do with that innocent man, for I have suffered a great deal today in a dream because of him."

Matthew 27:19

Women at the Cross: They Remained Faithful to Jesus

Among them were Mary Magdalene, Mary the mother of James and Joseph, and the mother of Zebedee's sons. As evening approached, there came a rich man from Arimathea, named Joseph, who had himself become a disciple of Jesus. Going to Pilate, he asked for Jesus' body, and Pilate ordered that it be given to him. Joseph took the body, wrapped it in a clean linen cloth, and placed it in his own new tomb that he had cut out of the rock. He rolled a big stone in front of the entrance to the tomb and went away. Mary Magdalene and the other Mary were sitting there across from the tomb.

Matthew 27:56-61

After the Sabbath, at dawn on the first day of the week, Mary Magdalene and the other Mary went to look at the tomb.

Matthew 28:1

Near the cross of Jesus stood his mother, his mother's sister, Mary the wife of Clopas, and Mary of Magdala.

John 19:25

When this had dawned on him, he went to the house of Mary the mother of John, also called Mark, where many people had gathered and were praying.

Acts 12:12

Lydia: She Became the First Convert in Europe
One of those listening was a woman named Lydia, a dealer in purple cloth from the city of Thyatira, who was a worshiper of God. The Lord opened her heart to respond to Paul's message. When she and the members of her household were baptized, she invited us to her home. "If you consider me a believer in

the Lord," she said, "come and stay at my house."
And she persuaded us.

Acts 16:14, 15

Priscilla and Phoebe: They Led in the Early Church

There he met a Jew named Aquila, a native of Pontus, who had recently come from Italy with his wife Priscilla, because Claudius had ordered all the Jews to leave Rome. Paul went to see them. . . .

Meanwhile a Jew named Apollos, a native of Alexandria, came to Ephesus. He was a learned man, with a thorough knowledge of the Scriptures. He had been instructed in the way of the Lord, and he spoke with great fervor and taught about Jesus accurately, though he knew only the baptism of John. He began to speak boldly in the synagogue. When Priscilla and Aquila heard him, they invited him to their home and explained to him the way of God more adequately.

Acts 18:2, 24-26

I commend to you our sister Phoebe, a servant of the church in Cenchrea. I ask you to receive her in the Lord in a way worthy of the saints and to give her any help she may need from you, for she has been a great help to many people, including me.

Romans 16:1, 2

FOR PERSONAL PRAYER:

Lord, sometimes I just get so tired. Help me to remember that my spiritual life is not failing just because I need a nap. Refresh me with a renewed sense of Your presence right now. Amen.

CHAPTER 2

'What if I've already made many mistakes parenting my kids?'

My goal is to be a perfect mom," says Julie. "But then I think: Just how realistic is that, really? I look back at some of the things I've done and I wonder if I've scarred my kids for life. They say they don't remember most of it, and they seem happy. But I still wish I could go back and do a few things over again.

"When I really get bothered by thoughts of failure, it helps to remember the Bible's emphasis on forgiveness and renewal. I also think it's helped to admit to my kids that I am not—and never will be in this life—perfect. Their respect for me grows when I sometimes have to ask their forgiveness, too."

FOR MEMORY:

May the words of my mouth and the meditation of my heart be pleasing in your sight, O LORD, my Rock and my Redeemer.

Psalm 19:14

FOR SILENT REFLECTION:

- *How honest am I with my kids about things I've done wrong?*

- *All in all, can I see that I've done a lot right, too?*

- *How do I view my standing with God when I feel that I've failed in some way?*

- *Can I refocus on my primary goal of leading my children to Christ and growth in Him?*

Heeding Proverbial Wisdom for Women

The woman Folly is loud; she is undisciplined and without knowledge.

Proverbs 9:13

A kindhearted woman gains respect, but ruthless men gain only wealth.

Proverbs 11:16

Like a gold ring in a pig's snout is a beautiful woman who shows no discretion.

Proverbs 11:22

The wise woman builds her house, but with her own hands the foolish one tears hers down.

Proverbs 14:1

Houses and wealth are inherited from parents, but a prudent wife is from the LORD.

Proverbs 19:14

A quarrelsome wife is like a constant dripping on a rainy day;

Proverbs 27:15

Mothers: Good Examples

They Modeled Faithfulness

I have been reminded of your sincere faith, which first lived in your grandmother Lois and in your mother Eunice and, I am persuaded, now lives in you also.

II Timothy 1:5

She Provided for A Prophet

One day Elisha went to Shunem. And a well-to-do woman was there, who urged him to stay for a meal. So whenever he came by, he stopped there to eat. She said to her husband, "I know that this man who often comes our way is a holy man of God. Let's make a small room on the roof and put in it a bed and a table, a chair and a lamp for him. Then he can stay there whenever he comes to us." . . .

"About this time next year," Elisha said, "you will hold a son in your arms." "No, my lord," she objected. "Don't mislead your servant, O man of God!" But the woman became pregnant, and the next year about that same time she gave birth to a son, just as Elisha had told her. The child grew, and one day he went out to his father, who was with the reapers. "My head! My head!" he said to his father. His father told a servant, "Carry him to his mother." After the servant had lifted him up and carried him to his mother, the boy sat on her lap until noon, and then he died. She went up and laid him on the bed of the man of God, then shut the door and went out. She called her husband and said, "Please send me one of the servants and a donkey so I can go to the man of God quickly and return." . . .

When Elisha reached the house, there was the boy lying dead on his couch. He went in, shut the door on the two of them and prayed to the LORD. Then he got on the bed and lay upon the boy, mouth to mouth, eyes to eyes, hands to hands. As he stretched himself out upon him, the boy's body grew warm. Elisha turned away and walked back and forth in the room and then got on the bed and stretched out upon him once more. The boy sneezed seven times and opened his eyes. Elisha summoned Gehazi and said, "Call the Shunammite." And he did. When she came, he said, "Take your son." She came in, fell at his feet and bowed to the ground. Then she took her son and went out.

II Kings 4:8-37

She Glorified the Lord

[An] angel went to [Mary] and said, "Greetings, you who are highly favored! The Lord is with you." Mary was greatly troubled at his words and wondered what kind of greeting this might be.

But the angel said to her, "Do not be afraid, Mary,

31

you have found favor with God. You will be with child and give birth to a son, and you are to give him the name Jesus. He will be great and will be called the Son of the Most High. The Lord God will give him the throne of his father David, and he will reign over the house of Jacob forever; his kingdom will never end." "How will this be," Mary asked the angel, "since I am a virgin?"

The angel answered, "The Holy Spirit will come upon you, and the power of the Most High will over-shadow you. So the holy one to be born will be called the Son of God. Even Elizabeth your relative is going to have a child in her old age, and she who was said to be barren is in her sixth month. For noth-ing is impossible with God."

"I am the Lord's servant," Mary answered. "May it be to me as you have said." Then the angel left her.

At that time Mary got ready and hurried to a town in the hill country of Judea, where she entered Zechariah's home and greeted Elizabeth. When Eliza-beth heard Mary's greeting, the baby leaped in her womb, and Elizabeth was filled with the Holy Spirit. In a loud voice she exclaimed: "Blessed are you among women, and blessed is the child you will bear!
. . .

And Mary said:

"My soul praises the Lord and my spirit rejoices in God my Savior, for he has been mindful of the humble state of his servant. From now on all generations will call me blessed, for the Mighty One has done great things for me—holy is his name. His mercy extends to those who fear him, from generation to generation. He has performed mighty deeds with his arm; he has scattered those who are proud in their inmost thoughts. He has brought down rulers from their thrones but has lifted up the humble. He has filled the hungry with good things but has sent the rich away empty. He has helped his servant Israel, remembering to be merciful to Abraham and his descendants forever, even as he said to our fathers."

Luke 1:28-55

She Proclaimed the Christ Child

There was also a prophetess, Anna, the daughter of Phanuel, of the tribe of Asher. She was very old; she had lived with her husband seven years after her marriage, and then was a widow until she was eighty-four. She never left the temple but worshiped night and day, fasting and praying. Coming up to them at that very moment, she gave thanks to God and spoke about the child to all who were looking forward to the redemption of Jerusalem.

Luke 2:36-38

Mothers: Bad Examples

She Encouraged Idolatry

Now a man named Micah from the hill country of Ephraim said to his mother, "The eleven hundred shekels of silver that were taken from you and about which I heard you utter a curse—I have that silver with me; I took it." Then his mother said, "The LORD bless you, my son!" When he returned the eleven hundred shekels of silver to his mother, she said, "I solemnly consecrate my silver to the LORD for my son to make a carved image and a cast idol. I will give it back to you." So he returned the silver to his mother, and she took two hundred shekels of silver and gave them to a silversmith, who made them into the image and the idol. And they were put in Micah's house.

Judges 17:1-4

They Valued Self-preservation Too highly

As the king of Israel was passing by on the wall, a woman cried to him, "Help me, my lord the king!" The king replied, "If the LORD does not help you, where can I get help for you? From the threshing floor? From the winepress?" Then he asked her, "What's the matter?" She answered, "This woman said to me, 'Give up your son so we may eat him today, and tomorrow we'll eat my son.' So we cooked my

son and ate him. The next day I said to her, 'Give up
your son so we may eat him,' but she had hidden
him." When the king heard the woman's words, he
tore his robes. As he went along the wall, the people
looked, and there, underneath, he had sackcloth on
his body.

II Kings 6:26-30

She Ruined Her Life with Greed

[Ahab's] wife Jezebel came in and asked him, "Why
are you so sullen? Why won't you eat?" He answered
her, "Because I said to Naboth the Jezreelite, 'Sell me
your vineyard; or if you prefer, I will give you another vineyard in its place.' But he said, 'I will not give
you my vineyard.'" Jezebel his wife said, "Is this how
you act as king over Israel? Get up and eat! Cheer
up. I'll get you the vineyard of Naboth the Jezreelite."
So she wrote letters in Ahab's name, placed his seal
on them, and sent them to the elders and nobles
who lived in Naboth's city with him. In those letters
she wrote: "Proclaim a day of fasting and seat
Naboth in a prominent place among the people. But
seat two scoundrels opposite him and have them tes-
tify that he has cursed both God and the king. Then
take him out and stone him to death." . . .

As soon as Jezebel heard that Naboth had been
stoned to death, she said to Ahab, "Get up and take
possession of the vineyard of Naboth the Jezreelite

that he refused to sell you. He is no longer alive, but dead." When Ahab heard that Naboth was dead, he got up and went down to take possession of Naboth's vineyard. Then the word of the LORD came to Elijah the Tishbite: . . .

"Concerning Jezebel the LORD says: 'Dogs will devour Jezebel by the wall of Jezreel.'

I Kings 21:5-23

Admitting Your Shortcomings with Your Kids

Who can discern [her] errors?
Forgive my hidden faults.
Keep your servant also from willful sins;
may they not rule over me.
Then will I be blameless,
innocent of great transgression.
May the words of my mouth and the meditation
of my heart be pleasing in your sight, O LORD,
my Rock and my Redeemer.

Psalm 19:12-14

"No one lights a lamp and puts it in a place where it will be hidden, or under a bowl. Instead he puts it on its stand, so that those who come in may see the light. Your eye is the lamp of your body. When your eyes are good, your whole body also is full of light. But when they are bad, your body also is full of darkness. See to it, then, that the light within you is not darkness. Therefore, if your whole body is full of light, and no part of it dark, it will be completely lighted, as when the light of a lamp shines on you."

Luke 11:33-36

There is nothing concealed that will not be disclosed, or hidden that will not be made known. What you have said in the dark will be heard in the daylight, and what you have whispered in the ear in the inner rooms will be proclaimed from the housetops.

Luke 12:2, 3

I know that nothing good lives in me, that is, in my sinful nature. For I have the desire to do what is good, but I cannot carry it out. For what I do is not the good I want to do; no, the evil I do not want to do—this I keep on doing. Now if I do what I do not want to do, it is no longer I who do it, but it is sin living in me that does it.

Romans 7:18-20

Leading Your Kids to Jesus

Come to me, all you who are weary and burdened, and I will give you rest. Take my yoke upon you and learn from me, for I am gentle and humble in heart, and you will find rest for your souls. For my yoke is

37

easy and my burden is light.

Matthew 11:28-30

At that time the disciples came to Jesus and asked, "Who is the greatest in the kingdom of heaven?" He called a little child and had him stand among them. And he said: "I tell you the truth, unless you change and become like little children, you will never enter the kingdom of heaven.

Therefore, whoever humbles himself like this child is the greatest in the kingdom of heaven. And whoever welcomes a little child like this in my name welcomes me. But if anyone causes one of these little ones who believe in me to sin, it would be better for him to have a large millstone hung around his neck and to be drowned in the depths of the sea.

Woe to the world because of the things that cause people to sin! Such things must come, but woe to the man through whom they come! If your hand or your foot causes you to sin cut it off and throw it away. It is better for you to enter life maimed or crippled than to have two hands or two feet and be thrown into eternal fire.

And if your eye causes you to sin, gouge it out and throw it away. It is better for you to enter life with one eye than to have two eyes and be thrown into the fire of hell. See that you do not look down on one of these little ones. For I tell you that their angels in heaven always see the face of my Father in heaven."

Matthew 18:1-10

On the last and greatest day of the Feast, Jesus stood and said in a loud voice, "If a man is thirsty, let him come to me and drink. Whoever believes in me, as the Scripture has said, streams of living water will flow from within him."

John 7:37, 38

You see, at just the right time, when we were still powerless, Christ died for the ungodly. Very rarely will anyone die for a righteous man, though for a good man someone might possibly dare to die. But God demonstrates his own love for us in this: While we were still sinners, Christ died for us. Since we have now been justified by his blood, how much more shall we be saved from God's wrath through him! For if, when we were God's enemies, we were reconciled to him through the death of his Son, how much more, having been reconciled, shall we be saved through his life!

Romans 5:6-10

[So] if you confess with your mouth, "Jesus is Lord," and believe in your heart that God raised him from the dead, you will be saved. For it is with your heart

that you believe and are justified, and it is with your
mouth that you confess and are saved.

Romans 10:9, 10

FOR PERSONAL PRAYER:

*Lord, I've tried to be a good mom so far, but I
know I've made many mistakes. Help me to
remember that the reason You came to earth
was to save sinners. That qualifies me as one of
your special projects. Praise to you, Lord! Amen.*

CHAPTER 3

'What if I'm having problems in my marriage?'

Someone once told me the best thing I could do for my children was to love their father," said LaVonne. "To me, that means a key part of my parenting responsibility is keeping my marriage strong and healthy. "

"I know it takes two people to make a marriage work, but I want to do my part the best I can. And I'm always inspired by the examples of godly wives I find in the Bible."

FOR MEMORY:

The wise woman builds her house, but with her own hands the foolish one tears hers down.

Proverbs 14:1

FOR SILENT REFLECTION:

- *How is my level of marital happiness affecting my children's feelings of security and contentment in the home?*

- *How would I assess the strength of my marriage right now?*

- *What things can I do better to make my marriage stronger?*

- *Where do I need God's help and strength the most to be the best wife I can be?*

Being a Virtuous Wife and Mother

A wife of noble character who can find?
She is worth far more than rubies.
Her husband has full confidence in her
and lacks nothing of value.
She brings him good, not harm,
all the days of her life.
She selects wool and flax
and works with eager hands.
She is like the merchant ships,
bringing her food from afar.
She gets up while it is still dark;
she provides food for her family
and portions for her servant girls.
She considers a field and buys it;
out of her earnings she plants a vineyard.
She sets about her work vigorously;
her arms are strong for her tasks.
She sees that her trading is profitable,
and her lamp does not go out at night.
In her hand she holds the distaff
and grasps the spindle with her fingers.
She opens her arms to the poor
and extends her hands to the needy.
When it snows, she has no fear for her household;
for all of them are clothed in scarlet.
She makes coverings for her bed;

she is clothed in fine linen and purple.
Her husband is respected at the city gate,
where he takes his seat among the elders of the land.
She makes linen garments and sells them,
and supplies the merchants with sashes.
She is clothed with strength and dignity;
she can laugh at the days to come.
She speaks with wisdom,
and faithful instruction is on her tongue.
She watches over the affairs of her household
and does not eat the bread of idleness.
Her children arise and call her blessed;
her husband also, and he praises her:
Many women do noble things,
but you surpass them all.
Charm is deceptive, and beauty is fleeting;
but a woman who fears the LORD is to be praised.
Give her the reward she has earned,
and let her works bring her praise at the city gate.

Proverbs 31:10-31

How beautiful you are, my darling!
Oh, how beautiful!
Your eyes behind your veil are doves.
Your hair is like a flock of goats
descending from Mount Gilead.
Your teeth are like a flock of sheep just shorn,
coming up from the washing.

Each has its twin; not one of them is alone.
Your lips are like a scarlet ribbon; your mouth is lovely.
Your temples behind your veil
are like the halves of a pomegranate.
Your neck is like the tower of David,
built with elegance; on it hang a thousand shields,
all of them shields of warriors.
Your two breasts are like two fawns,
like twin fawns of a gazelle
that browse among the lilies.
Until the day breaks and the shadows flee,
I will go to the mountain of myrrh
and to the hill of incense.
All beautiful you are, my darling;
there is no flaw in you.

Song of Songs 4:1-7

Some Good Examples

Manoah's Wife

A certain man of Zorah, named Manoah, from the clan of the Danites, had a wife who was sterile and remained childless. The angel of the LORD appeared to her and said, "You are sterile and childless, but you are going to conceive and have a son. Now see to it that you drink no wine or other fermented drink and that you do not eat anything unclean, because you will conceive and give birth to a son. No razor

45

may be used on his head, because the boy is to be a Nazirite, set apart to God from birth, and he will begin the deliverance of Israel from the hands of the Philistines."

Then the woman went to her husband and told him, "A man of God came to me. He looked like an angel of God, very awesome. I didn't ask him where he came from, and he didn't tell me his name. But he said to me, 'You will conceive and give birth to a son. Now then, drink no wine or other fermented drink and do not eat anything unclean, because the boy will be a Nazirite of God from birth until the day of his death.'"

Then Manoah prayed to the LORD: "O Lord, I beg you, let the man of God you sent to us come again to teach us how to bring up the boy who is to be born." God heard Manoah, and the angel of God came again to the woman while she was out in the field; but her husband Manoah was not with her.

The woman hurried to tell her husband, "He's here! The man who appeared to me the other day!" Manoah got up and followed his wife. When he came to the man, he said, "Are you the one who talked to my wife?" "I am," he said. So Manoah asked him, "When your words are fulfilled, what is to be the rule for the boy's life and work?"

The angel of the LORD answered, "Your wife must do all that I have told her. She must not eat anything that comes from the grapevine, nor drink any wine or other fermented drink nor eat anything unclean. She must do everything I have commanded her." . . . The woman gave birth to a boy and named him Samson. He grew and the LORD blessed him, and the Spirit of the LORD began to stir him.

Judges 13:2-25a

Wives of Sincere Faith

Paul, an apostle of Christ Jesus by the will of God, according to the promise of life that is in Christ Jesus, To Timothy, my dear son: Grace, mercy and peace from God the Father and Christ Jesus our Lord. I thank God, whom I serve, as my forefathers did, with a clear conscience, as night and day I constantly remember you in my prayers. Recalling your tears, I long to see you, so that I may be filled with joy. I have been reminded of your sincere faith, which first lived in your grandmother Lois and in your mother Eunice and, I am persuaded, now lives in you also.

II Timothy 1:1-5

Some Poor Examples

Potiphar's wife

After a while his master's wife took notice of Joseph and said, "Come to bed with me!" But he refused. "With me in charge," he told her, "my master does

47

not concern himself with anything in the house; everything he owns he has entrusted to my care. No one is greater in this house than I am. My master has withheld nothing from me except you, because you are his wife. How then could I do such a wicked thing and sin against God?" And though she spoke to Joseph day after day, he refused to go to bed with her or even be with her.

One day he went into the house to attend to his duties, and none of the household servants was inside. She caught him by his cloak and said, "Come to bed with me!" But he left his cloak in her hand and ran out of the house. When she saw that he had left his cloak in her hand and had run out of the house, she called her household servants. "Look," she said to them, "this Hebrew has been brought to us to make sport of us! He came in here to sleep with me, but I screamed. When he heard me scream for help, he left his cloak beside me and ran out of the house." She kept his cloak beside her until his master came home. Then she told him this story: "That Hebrew slave you brought us came to me to make sport of me. But as soon as I screamed for help, he left his cloak beside me and ran out of the house."

When his master heard the story his wife told him, saying, "This is how your slave treated me," he burned with anger.

Genesis 39:7-19

Samson's Wife

On the fourth day, they said to Samson's wife, "Coax your husband into explaining the riddle for us, or we will burn you and your father's household to death. Did you invite us here to rob us?" Then Samson's wife threw herself on him, sobbing, "You hate me! You don't really love me. You've given my people a riddle, but you haven't told me the answer." "I haven't even explained it to my father or mother," he replied, "so why should I explain it to you?"

She cried the whole seven days of the feast. So on the seventh day he finally told her, because she continued to press him. She in turn explained the riddle to her people.

Before sunset on the seventh day the men of the town said to him, "What is sweeter than honey? What is stronger than a lion?" Samson said to them, "If you had not plowed with my heifer, you would not have solved my riddle."

Then the Spirit of the LORD came upon him in power. He went down to Ashkelon, struck down thirty of their men, stripped them of their belongings and gave their clothes to those who had explained the riddle. Burning with anger, he went up to his father's house. And Samson's wife was given to the friend who had attended him at his wedding.

Judges 14:15-20

Providing a Nurturing Home Environment

Where Hospitality Reigns

For I was hungry and you gave me something to eat, I was thirsty and you gave me something to drink, I was a stranger and you invited me in, I needed clothes and you clothed me, I was sick and you looked after me, I was in prison and you came to visit me.'. . . "The King will reply, 'I tell you the truth, whatever you did for one of the least of these brothers of mine, you did for me.'

Matthew 25:35-40

I tell you the truth, anyone who gives you a cup of water in my name because you belong to Christ will certainly not lose his reward.

Mark 9:41

In everything I did, I showed you that by this kind of hard work we must help the weak, remembering the words the Lord Jesus himself said: 'It is more blessed to give than to receive.'

Acts 20:35

Share with God's people who are in need. Practice hospitality.

Romans 12:13

Our desire is not that others might be relieved while you are hard pressed, but that there might be equality. At the present time your plenty will supply what they need, so that in turn their plenty will supply what you need. Then there will be equality.

II Corinthians 8:13, 14

Suppose a brother or sister is without clothes and daily food. If one of you says to him, "Go, I wish you well; keep warm and well fed," but does nothing about his physical needs, what good is it?

James 2:15, 16

Offer hospitality to one another without grumbling. Each one should use whatever gift he has received to serve others, faithfully administering God's grace in its various forms.

I Peter 4:9, 10

If anyone has material possessions and sees his brother in need but has no pity on him, how can the love of God be in him?

I John 3:17

Do not forget to entertain strangers, for by so doing some people have entertained angels without knowing it.

Hebrews 13:2

Where Loving Talk Abounds

An offended brother is more unyielding than a forti-
fied city, and disputes are like the barred gates of a
citadel.

Proverbs 18:19

A foolish son is his father's ruin, and a quarrelsome
wife is like a constant dripping.

Proverbs 19:13

Better to live on a corner of the roof than share a
house with a quarrelsome wife.

Proverbs 21:9

May the God who gives endurance and encourage-
ment give you a spirit of unity among yourselves as
you follow Christ Jesus, so that with one heart and
mouth you may glorify the God and Father of our
Lord Jesus Christ.

Romans 15:5, 6

Carry each other's burdens, and in this way you will
fulfill the law of Christ. If anyone thinks he is something when he is nothing, he deceives himself. Each
one should test his own actions. Then he can take
pride in himself, without comparing himself to some-
body else.

Galatians 6:2-4

Be completely humble and gentle; be patient, bearing with one another in love. Make every effort to keep the unity of the Spirit through the bond of peace.

Ephesians 4:2, 3

Speaking the truth in love, we will in all things grow up into him who is the Head, that is, Christ. From him the whole body, joined and held together by every supporting ligament, grows and builds itself up in love, as each part does its work.

Ephesians 4:15, 16

Speak to one another with psalms, hymns and spiritual songs. Sing and make music in your heart to the Lord, always giving thanks to God the Father for everything, in the name of our Lord Jesus Christ.

Ephesians 5:19, 20

Where God Is Honored

Know therefore that the LORD your God is God; he is the faithful God, keeping his covenant of love to a thousand generations of those who love him and keep his commands.

Deuteronomy 7:9

So if you faithfully obey the commands I am giving

53

you today—to love the LORD your God and to serve him with all your heart and with all your soul— then I will send rain on your land in its season, both autumn and spring rains, so that you may gather in your grain, new wine and oil. I will provide grass in the fields for your cattle, and you will eat and be satisfied.

Deuteronomy 11:13-15

Delight yourself in the LORD and he will give you the desires of your heart.

Psalm 37:4

The LORD watches over all who love him, but all the wicked he will destroy.

Psalm 145:20

I love those who love me, and those who seek me find me.

Proverbs 8:17

Whoever has my commands and obeys them, he is the one who loves me. He who loves me will be loved by my Father, and I too will love him and show myself to him.

John 14:21

Keeping Your Marriage Strong

My lover is radiant and ruddy,
outstanding among ten thousand.
His head is purest gold;
his hair is wavy and black as a raven.
His eyes are like doves by the water streams,
 washed in milk, mounted like jewels.
His cheeks are like beds of spice yielding perfume.
His lips are like lilies dripping with myrrh. His arms
are rods of gold set with chrysolite. His body is like
polished ivory decorated with sapphires. His legs are
pillars of marble set on bases of pure gold.
His appearance is like Lebanon, choice as its cedars.
His mouth is sweetness itself;
he is altogether lovely.
This is my lover, this my friend,
O daughters of Jerusalem.

Song of Songs 5:10-16

Submit to one another out of reverence for Christ. . . .
Husbands, love your wives, just as Christ loved the
church and gave himself up for her to make her holy,
cleansing her by the washing with water through the
word, and to present her to himself as a radiant
church, without stain or wrinkle or any other blemish,
but holy and blameless. In this same way, husbands
ought to love their wives as their own bodies.

He who loves his wife loves himself. After all, no one ever hated his own body, but he feeds and cares for it, just as Christ does the church— for we are members of his body. "For this reason a man will leave his father and mother and be united to his wife, and the two will become one flesh."

This is a profound mystery—but I am talking about Christ and the church. However, each one of you also must love his wife as he loves himself.

Ephesians 5:21-33a

To the married I give this command (not I, but the Lord): A wife must not separate from her husband. But if she does, she must remain unmarried or else be reconciled to her husband. And a husband must not divorce his wife.

To the rest I say this (I, not the Lord): If any brother has a wife who is not a believer and she is willing to live with him, he must not divorce her. And if a woman has a husband who is not a believer and he is willing to live with her, she must not divorce him. For the unbelieving husband has been sanctified through his wife, and the unbelieving wife has been sanctified through her believing husband. Otherwise your children would be unclean, but as it is, they are holy. But if the unbeliever leaves, let him do so.

A believing man or woman is not bound in such

circumstances; God has called us to live in peace. How do you know, wife, whether you will save your husband? Or, how do you know, husband, whether you will save your wife?

I Corinthians 7:10-16

Wives, submit to your husbands as to the Lord. For the husband is the head of the wife as Christ is the head of the church, his body, of which he is the Savior. Now as the church submits to Christ, so also wives should submit to their husbands in everything.

Ephesians 5:22-24

Teach the older women to be reverent in the way they live, not to be slanderers or addicted to much wine, but to teach what is good. Then they can train the younger women to love their husbands and children, to be self-controlled and pure, to be busy at home, to be kind, and to be subject to their husbands, so that no one will malign the word of God.

Titus 2:3-5

FOR PERSONAL PRAYER:

Lord, I give you my marriage. Grow both my husband and me into whole persons so that we can enjoy each other wholly. Help me find fulfillment with my own plans and dreams, too—not expecting my husband to meet all my needs. Let our love for each other overflow into the lives of our kids. Amen.

CHAPTER 4

'How can I help revitalize my family's spiritual life?'

When I think about the real priorities that come through in my family, it seems like prayer and reading the Bible come last on everybody's list," says Sarah. "It's not that we consciously ignore our spiritual life as a family, it's just that it usually gets pushed to the side because of time pressures or lack of energy. "Something else always comes up when we plan to sit down together with God's Word. Maybe it just seems easier to sit in front of the TV than to sit in front of the Lord for awhile."

FOR MEMORY:

Do not let this Book of the Law depart from your mouth; meditate on it day and night, so that you may be careful to do everything written in it. Then you will be prosperous and successful.

Joshua 1:8

FOR SILENT REFLECTION:

- *Do my children value the Bible and prayer?*

- *To what extent have my kids' spiritual attitudes been formed by observing my own priorities?*

- *What are my personal prayer habits?*

- *What practical steps can I take to introduce prayer into my kids' lives?*

Give Your Children a Love for God's Word

I will meditate on all your works and consider all
your mighty deeds.

Psalm 77:12

On my bed I remember you; I think of you through
the watches of the night.

Psalm 63:6

I have hidden your word in my heart
that I might not sin against you. . . .
I delight in your decrees;
I will not neglect your word. . . .
Then I will answer the one who taunts me,
for I trust in your word. . . .
My comfort in my suffering is this:
Your promise preserves my life.

Psalm 119:11-50

I remember the days of long ago; I meditate on all
your works and consider what your hands have
done.

Psalm 143:5

Your word is a lamp to my feet
and a light for my path. . . .
Sustain me according to your promise,

and I will live; do not let my hopes be dashed. . . .
Direct my footsteps according to your word;
let no sin rule over me. . . .
Your promises have been thoroughly tested,
and your servant loves them. . . .
I rise before dawn and cry for help;
I have put my hope in your word.
My eyes stay open through the watches of the night,
that I may meditate on your promises. . . .
Defend my cause and redeem me;
preserve my life according to your promise.

Psalm 119:105-154

Finally, brothers, whatever is true, whatever is noble,
whatever is right, whatever is pure, whatever is lovely, whatever is admirable—if anything is excellent or
praiseworthy—think about such things.

Philippians 4:8

For the word of God is living and active. Sharper
than any double-edged sword, it penetrates even to
dividing soul and spirit, joints and marrow; it judges
the thoughts and attitudes of the heart. Nothing in all
creation is hidden from God's sight. Everything is
uncovered and laid bare before the eyes of him to
whom we must give account.

Hebrews 4:12, 13

Be diligent in these matters; give yourself wholly to them, so that everyone may see your progress.

I Timothy 4:15

All Scripture is God-breathed and is useful for teaching, rebuking, correcting and training in righteousness. So that the man of God may be thoroughly equipped for every good work.

II Timothy 3:16, 17

Teach Your Children to Pray

Pray continually.

I Thessalonians 5:17

"Why are you sleeping?" he asked them. "Get up and pray so that you will not fall into temptation."

Luke 22:46

Through Jesus, therefore, let us continually offer to God a sacrifice of praise—the fruit of lips that confess his name.

Hebrews 13:15

The end of all things is near. Therefore be clear minded and self-controlled so that you can pray.

I Peter 4:7

63

And pray in the Spirit on all occasions with all kinds of prayers and requests. With this in mind, be alert and always keep on praying for all the saints.

Ephesians 6:18

Let us draw near to God with a sincere heart in full assurance of faith, having our hearts sprinkled to cleanse us from a guilty conscience and having our bodies washed with pure water.

Hebrews 10:22

Ask and it will be given to you; seek and you will find; knock and the door will be opened to you. For everyone who asks receives; he who seeks finds; and to him who knocks, the door will be opened. Which of you, if his son asks for bread, will give him a stone? Or if he asks for a fish, will give him a snake? If you, then, though you are evil, know how to give good gifts to your children, how much more will your Father in heaven give good gifts to those who ask him!

Matthew 7:7-11

I tell you the truth, whatever you bind on earth will be bound in heaven, and whatever you loose on earth will be loosed in heaven. Again, I tell you that if two of you on earth agree about anything you ask for, it will be done for you by my Father in heaven.

For where two or three come together in my name, there am I with them.

Matthew 18:18-20

"Have faith in God," Jesus answered. "I tell you the truth, if anyone says to this mountain, 'Go, throw yourself into the sea,' and does not doubt in his heart but believes that what he says will happen, it will be done for him.

Mark 11:22, 23

If you remain in me and my words remain in you, ask whatever you wish, and it will be given you. This is to my Father's glory, that you bear much fruit, showing yourselves to be my disciples. As the Father has loved me, so have I loved you. Now remain in my love. If you obey my commands, you will remain in my love, just as I have obeyed my Father's commands and remain in his love. I have told you this so that my joy may be in you and that your joy may be complete.

My command is this: Love each other as I have loved you. Greater love has no one than this, that he lay down his life for his friends. You are my friends if you do what I command. I no longer call you servants, because a servant does not know his master's business. Instead, I have called you friends, for everything that I learned from my Father I have made known to you. You did not choose me, but I chose you to go and bear fruit—fruit that will last. Then the Father will give you whatever you ask in my name.

John 15:7-16

Their Father Hears

This is the assurance we have in approaching God: that if we ask anything according to his will, he hears us.

I John 5:14

Call to me and I will answer you and tell you great and unsearchable things you do not know.

Jeremiah 33:3

If any of you lacks wisdom, he should ask God, who gives generously to all without finding fault, and it will be given to him.

James 1:5

Then Hannah prayed and said: "My heart rejoices in the LORD; in the LORD my horn is lifted high. My mouth boasts over my enemies, for I delight in your deliverance. . . .And the LORD was gracious to Hannah; she conceived and gave birth to three sons and two daughters. Meanwhile, the boy Samuel grew up in the presence of the LORD.

I Samuel 2:1, 21

If my people, who are called by my name, will humble themselves and pray and seek my face and turn from their wicked ways, then will I hear from heaven and will forgive their sin and will heal their land.

II Chronicles 7:14

Yet if you devote your heart to him and stretch out your hands to him, if you put away the sin that is in your hand and allow no evil to dwell in your tent, then you will lift up your face without shame; you will stand firm and without fear. You will surely forget your trouble, recalling it only as waters gone by. Life will be brighter than noonday, and darkness will become like morning. You will be secure, because there is hope; you will look about you and take your rest in safety. You will lie down, with no one to make you afraid, and many will court your favor.

Job 11:13-19

The LORD is near to all who call on him, to all who call on him in truth. He fulfills the desires of those who fear him; he hears their cry and saves them.

-Psalm 145:18, 19

Then you will call, and the LORD will answer; you will cry for help, and he will say: Here am I. If you do away with the yoke of oppression, with the pointing finger and malicious talk.

Isaiah 58:9

But when you pray, go into your room, close the door and pray to your Father, who is unseen. Then your Father, who sees what is done in secret, will reward you. And when you pray, do not keep on babbling like pagans, for they think they will be heard because of their many words. Do not be like them, for your Father knows what you need before you ask him. This, then, is how you should pray:

Our Father in heaven, hallowed be your name, your kingdom come, your will be done on earth as it is in heaven. Give us today our daily bread. Forgive us our debts, as we also have forgiven our debtors. And lead us not into temptation, but deliver us from the evil one.

Matthew 6:6-13

Their Savior Prays for Them

But I have prayed for you, Simon, that your faith may not fail. And when you have turned back, strengthen your brothers."

Luke 22:32

I pray for them. I am not praying for the world, but for those you have given me, for they are yours. All I have is yours, and all you have is mine. And glory has come to me through them. I will remain in the world no longer, but they are still in the world, and I am coming to you. Holy Father, protect them by the power of your name—the name you gave me—so that they may be one as we are one. While I was with them, I protected them and kept them safe by that name you gave me. None has been lost except the one doomed to destruction so that Scripture would be fulfilled. "I am coming to you now, but I say these things while I am still in the world, so that they may have the full measure of my joy within them. I have given them your word and the world has hated them, for they are not of the world any more than I am of the world. My prayer is not that you take them out of the world but that you protect them from the evil one.

John 17:9-15

Therefore he is able to save completely those who come to God through him, because he always lives to intercede for them.

Hebrews 7:25

For Christ did not enter a man-made sanctuary that was only a copy of the true one; he entered heaven itself, now to appear for us in God's presence.

Hebrews 9:24

My dear children, I write this to you so that you will not sin. But if anybody does sin, we have one who speaks to the Father in our defense—Jesus Christ, the Righteous One.

1 John 2:1

Their Lord Helps Against Temptation

The tempter came to him and said, "If you are the Son of God, tell these stones to become bread." Jesus answered, "It is written: 'Man does not live on bread alone, but on every word that comes from the mouth of God.'" Then the devil took him to the holy city and had him stand on the highest point of the temple. "If you are the Son of God," he said, "throw yourself down.

For it is written: "'He will command his angels concerning you, and they will lift you up in their hands, so that you will not strike your foot against a stone.'" Jesus answered him, "It is also written: 'Do not put the Lord your God to the test.'" Again, the devil took him to a very high mountain and showed him all the kingdoms of the world and their splendor. All this I will give you," he said, "if you will bow down and worship me." Jesus said to him, "Away from me, Satan! For it is written: 'Worship the Lord your God, and serve him only.'" Then the devil left him, and angels came and attended him.

Matthew 4:3-11

Because he himself suffered when he was tempted, he is able to help those who are being tempted.

Hebrews 2:18

For we do not have a high priest who is unable to sympathize with our weaknesses, but we have one who has been tempted in every way, just as we are—yet was without sin.

Hebrews 4:15

Their Comforter Stays with Them

And I will do whatever you ask in my name, so that the Son may bring glory to the Father. You may ask me for anything in my name, and I will do it. If you love me, you will obey what I command. And I will ask the Father, and he will give you another Counselor to be with you forever— the Spirit of truth. The world cannot accept him, because it neither sees him nor knows him. But you know him, for he lives with you and will be in you.

John 14:13-17

All this I have spoken while still with you. But the Counselor, the Holy Spirit, whom the Father will send in my name, will teach you all things and will remind you of everything I have said to you. Peace I leave with you; my peace I give you. I do not give to you as the world gives. Do not let your hearts be

71

troubled and do not be afraid.

John 14:25-27

Now I am going to him who sent me, yet none of you asks me, 'Where are you going?' Because I have said these things, you are filled with grief. But I tell you the truth: It is for your good that I am going away. Unless I go away, the Counselor will not come to you; but if I go, I will send him to you.

When he comes, he will convict the world of guilt in regard to sin and righteousness and judgment: in regard to sin, because men do not believe in me; in regard to righteousness, because I am going to the Father, where you can see me no longer; and in regard to judgment, because the prince of this world now stands condemned.

I have much more to say to you, more than you can now bear. But when he, the Spirit of truth, comes, he will guide you into all truth. He will not speak on his own; he will speak only what he hears, and he will tell you what is yet to come. He will bring glory to me by taking from what is mine and making it known to you. All that belongs to the Father is mine. That is why I said the Spirit will take from what is mine and make it known to you.

John 16:5-15

FOR PERSONAL PRAYER:

Lord, I need to be convinced that nothing is more important than a close walk with you everyday. Show me that real success means coming to the end of the day knowing that I have been led by Your Spirit. And remind me that my children are watching to see if I really practice what I preach. Amen.

CHAPTER 5

'How can I raise my child's self-esteem when I suffer low self-esteem myself?'

I want my kids to like themselves and feel good about themselves," Cheryl said, "and to know that God views them as valuable and worthy of His love. But I still struggle with my own feelings of unworthiness.

"I've come to see that being a good mom includes working on building my own self-esteem so I can pass that on to my kids."

> **FOR MEMORY:**
> I praise you because I am fearfully and wonderfully made; your works are wonderful, I know that full well.
>
> *Psalm 139:14*

FOR SILENT REFLECTION:

- *Do I like who I am right now? Why, or why not?*

- *Which things about myself need to be changed and which need to be simply accepted?*

- *To what level do my kids sense that I love them unconditionally?*

- *Do I have a deep sense of God's unconditional love for ME?*

Do You or your Children Feel Unworthy of Love?

Moses Felt Unworthy

Now Moses was tending the flock of Jethro his father-in-law, the priest of Midian, and he led the flock to the far side of the desert and came to Horeb, the mountain of God. There the angel of the LORD appeared to him in flames of fire from within a bush. Moses saw that though the bush was on fire it did not burn up. So Moses thought, "I will go over and see this strange sight—why the bush does not burn up." When the LORD saw that he had gone over to look, God called to him from within the bush, "Moses! Moses!" And Moses said, "Here I am."

"Do not come any closer," God said. "Take off your sandals, for the place where you are standing is holy ground." Then he said, "I am the God of your father, the God of Abraham, the God of Isaac and the God of Jacob." At this, Moses hid his face, because he was afraid to look at God. The LORD said, "I have indeed seen the misery of my people in Egypt. I have heard them crying out because of their slave drivers, and I am concerned about their suffering. So I have come down to rescue them from the hand of the Egyptians and to bring them up out of that land into a good and spacious land, a land flowing with milk and honey—the home of the Canaanites, Hittites, Amorites, Perizzites, Hivites and Jebusites. And now the cry of the Israelites has reached me, and I have seen the way the Egyptians are oppressing them. So now, go. I am sending you to Pharaoh to bring my people the Israelites out of Egypt."

But Moses said to God, "Who am I, that I should go to Pharaoh and bring the Israelites out of Egypt?"

Exodus 3:1-11

Mephibosheth Felt Unworthy, Too

The king asked, "Is there no one still left of the house of Saul to whom I can show God's kindness?" Ziba answered the king, "There is still a son of Jonathan; he is crippled in both feet." . . .

When Mephibosheth son of Jonathan, the son of Saul, came to David, he bowed down to pay him honor. David said, "Mephibosheth!" "Your servant," he replied. "Don't be afraid," David said to him, "for I will surely show you kindness for the sake of your father Jonathan. I will restore to you all the land that belonged to your grandfather Saul, and you will always eat at my table."

Mephibosheth bowed down and said, "What is your servant, that you should notice a dead dog like me?"

II Samuel 9:3-8

Seeing Ourselves As Worthy Children

We Were Created in God's Image, and Honored

So God created man in his own image, in the image of God he created him; male and female he created them. God blessed them and said to them, "Be fruitful and increase in number; fill the earth and subdue it. Rule over the fish of the sea and the birds of the air and over every living creature that moves on the ground." Then God said, "I give you every seed-bearing plant on the face of the whole earth and every tree that has fruit with seed in it. They will be yours for food. And to all the beasts of the earth and all the birds of the air and all the creatures that move on the ground—everything that has the breath of life in it—I give every green plant for food." And it was so.

God saw all that he had made, and it was very good.

Genesis 1:27-31a

I praise you because I am fearfully
and wonderfully made;
your works are wonderful,
I know that full well.
My frame was not hidden from you
when I was made in the secret place.
When I was woven together

in the depths of the earth,
your eyes saw my unformed body.
All the days ordained for me
were written in your book
before one of them came to be.

Psalm 139:14-16

O LORD, our Lord,
how majestic is your name in all the earth!
You have set your glory above the heavens.
From the lips of children and infants
you have ordained praise because of your enemies,
to silence the foe and the avenger.
When I consider your heavens,
the work of your fingers,
the moon and the stars,
which you have set in place,
what is man that you are mindful of him,
the son of man that you care for him?
You made him a little lower than the heavenly
beings
and crowned him with glory and honor.
You made him ruler over the works of your hands;
you put everything under his feet:
all flocks and herds, and the beasts of the field,
the birds of the air, and the fish of the sea,
all that swim the paths of the seas.
O LORD, our Lord,

how majestic is your name in all the earth!

Psalm 8:1-9

We Were Born To Carry Out God's Will

Therefore go and make disciples of all nations, baptizing them in the name of the Father and of the Son and of the Holy Spirit, and teaching them to obey everything I have commanded you. And surely I am with you always, to the very end of the age."

Matthew 28:19, 20

Therefore, if anyone is in Christ, he is a new creation; the old has gone, the new has come! All this is from God, who reconciled us to himself through Christ and gave us the ministry of reconciliation: that God was reconciling the world to himself in Christ, not counting men's sins against them. And he has committed to us the message of reconciliation. We are therefore Christ's ambassadors, as though God were making his appeal through us. We implore you on Christ's behalf: Be reconciled to God.

II Corinthians 5:17-20

For we are God's workmanship, created in Christ Jesus to do good works, which God prepared in advance for us to do.

Ephesians 2:10

81

And we pray this in order that you may live a life worthy of the Lord and may please him in every way: bearing fruit in every good work, growing in the knowledge of God, being strengthened with all power according to his glorious might so that you may have great endurance and patience, and joyfully giving thanks to the Father, who has qualified you to share in the inheritance of the saints in the kingdom of light.

Colossians 1:10-12

We Are Considered Blameless Before God

To him who is able to keep you from falling and to present you before his glorious presence without fault and with great joy—to the only God our Savior be glory, majesty, power and authority, through Jesus Christ our Lord, before all ages, now and forevermore! Amen.

Jude 1:24, 25

The LORD has dealt with me according to my righteousness; according to the cleanness of my hands he has rewarded me. For I have kept the ways of the LORD; I have not done evil by turning from my God.

All his laws are before me; I have not turned away from his decrees. I have been blameless before him and have kept myself from sin. The LORD has rewarded me according to my righteousness, according to my cleanness in his sight. To the faithful you show yourself faithful, to the blameless you show yourself blameless, to the pure you show yourself pure.

II Samuel 22:21-27a

Praise be to the LORD,
for he showed his wonderful love to me
when I was in a besieged city.
In my alarm I said,
"I am cut off from your sight!"
Yet you heard my cry for mercy
when I called to you for help.
Love the LORD, all his saints!
The LORD preserves the faithful,
but the proud he pays back in full.
Be strong and take heart,
all you who hope in the LORD.

Psalm 31:21-24

But Jesus went to the Mount of Olives. At dawn he appeared again in the temple courts, where all the people gathered around him, and he sat down to teach them. The teachers of the law and the Pharisees brought in a woman caught in adultery.

They made her stand before the group and said to Jesus, "Teacher, this woman was caught in the act of adultery. In the Law Moses commanded us to stone such women. Now what do you say?" They were using this question as a trap, in order to have a basis for accusing him.

But Jesus bent down and started to write on the ground with his finger. When they kept on questioning him, he straightened up and said to them, "If any one of you is without sin, let him be the first to throw a stone at her."

Again he stooped down and wrote on the ground. At this, those who heard began to go away one at a time, the older ones first, until only Jesus was left, with the woman still standing there. Jesus straightened up and asked her, "Woman, where are they? Has no one condemned you?"

"No one, sir," she said.

"Then neither do I condemn you," Jesus declared. "Go now and leave your life of sin."

John 8:1-11

Therefore, there is now no condemnation for those who are in Christ Jesus, because through Christ Jesus the law of the Spirit of life set me free from the law of sin and death. For what the law was powerless to do in that it was weakened by the sinful nature, God did by sending his own Son in the likeness of sinful man to be a sin offering. And so he condemned sin in sinful man, in order that the righteous requirements of the law might be fully met in us, who do

not live according to the sinful nature but according
to the Spirit.

Romans 8:1-4

This then is how we know that we belong to the
truth, and how we set our hearts at rest in his presence whenever our hearts condemn us. For God is
greater than our hearts, and he knows everything.
Dear friends, if our hearts do not condemn us, we
have confidence before God.

I John 3:19-21

May God himself, the God of peace, sanctify you
through and through. May your whole spirit, soul
and body be kept blameless at the coming of our
Lord Jesus Christ. The one who calls you is faithful
and he will do it.

I Thessalonians 5:23, 24

God Promises His Children Temporal Blessings

He who dwells in the shelter of the Most High
will rest in the shadow of the Almighty.
will say of the LORD,
"He is my refuge and my fortress,
my God, in whom I trust."
Surely he will save you from the fowler's snare
and from the deadly pestilence.

He will cover you with his feathers,
and under his wings you will find refuge;
his faithfulness will be your shield and rampart.
You will not fear the terror of night,
nor the arrow that flies by day,
nor the pestilence that stalks in the darkness,
nor the plague that destroys at midday.
A thousand may fall at your side,
ten thousand at your right hand,
but it will not come near you.
You will only observe with your eyes
and see the punishment of the wicked.
If you make the Most High your dwelling—
even the LORD, who is my refuge—
then no harm will befall you,
no disaster will come near your tent.
For he will command his angels concerning you
to guard you in all your ways;
they will lift you up in their hands,
so that you will not strike your foot against a stone.
You will tread upon the lion and the cobra;
you will trample the great lion and the serpent.
"Because he loves me," says the LORD,
"I will rescue him; I will protect him,
for he acknowledges my name.
He will call upon me, and I will answer him;
I will be with him in trouble,
I will deliver him and honor him.

With long life will I satisfy him
and show him my salvation."

Psalm 91:1-16

And my God will meet all your needs according to
his glorious riches in Christ Jesus.

Philippians 4:19

Promises of Spiritual Blessing from God

I am the LORD your God, who brought you up out
of Egypt. Open wide your mouth and I will fill it.

Psalm 81:10

Blessed are those whose strength is in you, who
have set their hearts on pilgrimage.

Psalm 84:5

Then your light will break forth like the dawn,
and your healing will quickly appear;
then your righteousness will go before you,
and the glory of the LORD will be your rear guard.
Then you will call, and the LORD will answer;
you will cry for help, and he will say: Here am I.
"If you do away with the yoke of oppression,
with the pointing finger and malicious talk,
and if you spend yourselves on behalf of the hungry

and satisfy the needs of the oppressed,
then your light will rise in the darkness,
and your night will become like the noonday.
The LORD will guide you always;
he will satisfy your needs in a sun-scorched land
and will strengthen your frame.
You will be like a well-watered garden,
like a spring whose waters never fail.

Isaiah 58:8-11

They will come and shout for joy
on the heights of Zion;
they will rejoice in the bounty of the LORD—
the grain, the new wine and the oil,
the young of the flocks and herds.
They will be like a well-watered garden,
and they will sorrow no more.
Then maidens will dance and be glad,
young men and old as well.
I will turn their mourning into gladness;
I will give them comfort and joy instead of sorrow.
I will satisfy the priests with abundance,
and my people will be filled with my bounty,"
declares the LORD.

Jeremiah 31:12-14

If you then, though you are evil, know how to
give good gifts to your children, how much more

will your Father in heaven give the Holy Spirit to those who ask him!"

Luke 11:13

On the last and greatest day of the Feast, Jesus stood and said in a loud voice, "If anyone is thirsty, let him come to me and drink. Whoever believes in me, as the Scripture has said, streams of living water will flow from within him." By this he meant the Spirit, whom those who believed in him were later to receive. Up to that time the Spirit had not been given, since Jesus had not yet been glorified.

John 7:37-39

And I will ask the Father, and he will give you another Counselor to be with you forever—the Spirit of truth. The world cannot accept him, because it neither sees him nor knows him. But you know him, for he lives with you and will be in you. . . . But the Counselor, the Holy Spirit, whom the Father will send in my name, will teach you all things and will remind you of everything I have said to you. Peace I leave with you; my peace I give you. I do not give to you as the world gives. Do not let your hearts be troubled and do not be afraid.

John 14:16-27

Now I commit you to God and to the word of his

89

grace, which can build you up and give you an inheritance among all those who are sanctified.

Acts 20:32

To him who is able to keep you from falling and to present you before his glorious presence without fault and with great joy—to the only God our Savior be glory, majesty, power and authority, through Jesus Christ our Lord, before all ages, now and forevermore! Amen.

Jude 1:24, 25

God Will Lovingly Crown His Children

Everyone who competes in the games goes into strict training. They do it to get a crown that will not last; but we do it to get a crown that will last forever.

I Corinthians 9:25

Now there is in store for me the crown of righteousness, which the Lord, the righteous Judge, will award to me on that day—and not only to me, but also to all who have longed for his appearing.

II Timothy 4:8

Blessed is the man who perseveres under trial, because when he has stood the test, he will receive the crown of life that God has promised to those who love him.

James 1:12

And when the Chief Shepherd appears, you will receive the crown of glory that will never fade away.

I Peter 5:4

Do not be afraid of what you are about to suffer. I tell you, the devil will put some of you in prison to test you, and you will suffer persecution for ten days. Be faithful, even to the point of death, and I will give you the crown of life.

Revelation 2:10

We Can Bless Our Children, Too, By Saying:

Blessed are you (_____Your Child's Name_____),
when you do not walk in the counsel of the wicked
or stand in the way of sinners
or sit in the seat of mockers.
But your delight is in the law of the LORD,
and on his law may you meditate day and night.
Then you will be like a tree
planted by streams of water,
which yields its fruit in season
and whose leaf does not wither.
Whatever you do will prosper.
Not so the wicked!
They are like chaff that the wind blows away.

Therefore the wicked will not stand in the judgment,
nor sinners in the assembly of the righteous.
For the LORD watches over the way of the righteous,
but the way of the wicked will perish.

Psalm 1:1-6

My son/daughter, (_____ Name _____),
if you accept my words
and store up my commands within you,
turning your ear to wisdom
and applying your heart to understanding,
and if you call out for insight
and cry aloud for understanding,
and if you look for it as for silver
and search for it as for hidden treasure,
then you will understand the fear of the LORD
and find the knowledge of God.
For the LORD gives wisdom,
and from his mouth come
knowledge and understanding.
He holds victory in store for the upright,
he is a shield to those whose walk is blameless,
for he guards the course of the just
and protects the way of his faithful ones.

Proverbs 2:1-8

Trust in the LORD with all your heart, (_____ Name _____),
and lean not on your own understanding;

in all your ways acknowledge him,
and he will make your paths straight.

Proverbs 3:5, 6

I keep asking that the God of our Lord Jesus Christ, the glorious Father, may give you, (____Name____), the Spirit of wisdom and revelation, so that you may know him better. I pray also that the eyes of your heart may be enlightened in order that you may know the hope to which he has called you, the riches of his glorious inheritance in the saints, and his incomparably great power for us who believe. That power is like the working of his mighty strength, which he exerted in Christ when he raised him from the dead and seated him at his right hand in the heavenly realms, far above all rule and authority, power and dominion, and every title that can be given, not only in the present age but also in the one to come. And God placed all things under his feet and appointed him to be head over everything for the church, which is his body, the fullness of him who fills everything in every way.

Ephesians 1:17-23

I pray that out of his glorious riches [God] may strengthen you, (____Name____), with power through his Spirit in your inner being, so that Christ may dwell in your hearts through faith. And I pray that

93

you, being rooted and established in love, may have power, together with all the saints, to grasp how wide and long and high and deep is the love of Christ, and to know this love that surpasses knowledge—that you may be filled to the measure of all the fullness of God.

Ephesians 3:16-19

FOR PERSONAL PRAYER:

Lord, remind me that there is nothing I can do to make You love me any more or less than You already love me. Point me back to the Cross, where Your unconditional acceptance of me was eternally purchased with Your Son's blood. May I pass along complete acceptance to my children every day. Amen.

= Chapter 6 =

'How can I get my kids to mind me better?'

Linda explains: "It's essential to see discipline as a training task. I can't expect my kids to do the right things if they haven't been taught the clear difference between right and wrong.

"That's why I believe I've got to view myself as a teacher first and a disciplinarian second. I've found that when my kids know exactly what I'm expecting out of them, they are pretty content to make an attempt at it. Unconditional love does not rule out correction. But there's no doubt in my mind that clear instruction has avoided a lot of unnecessary punishment."

FOR MEMORY:
Do not forsake your mother's teaching.
Proverbs 6:20b

FOR SILENT REFLECTION:

- *Do I think ahead to help my kids avoid potential trouble or misbehavior?*

- *Or do I just wait to respond "after the fact" with punishment?*

- *What informal means of teaching and training would help my children better recognize God's will in their lives?*

Help Children See Respect as Their Duty

Each of you must respect his mother and father, and you must observe my Sabbaths. I am the LORD your God.

Leviticus 19:3

Honor your father and your mother, as the LORD your God has commanded you, so that you may live long and that it may go well with you in the land the LORD your God is giving you.

Deuteronomy 5:16

Do not forsake your mother's teaching.

Proverbs 6:20b

Children, obey your parents in everything, for this pleases the Lord.

Colossians 3:20

My son, if your heart is wise,
then my heart will be glad;
my inmost being will rejoice
when your lips speak what is right. . . .
Listen to your father, who gave you life,
and do not despise your mother when she is old. . . .
The father of a righteous man has great joy;
he who has a wise son delights in him.

97

May your father and mother be glad;
may she who gave you birth rejoice!
My son, give me your heart
and let your eyes keep to my ways.

Proverbs 23:15-26

Discipline Begins with Proper Teaching

Be careful, and watch yourselves closely so that you
do not forget the things your eyes have seen or let
them slip from your heart as long as you live. Teach
them to your children and to their children after
them. Remember the day you stood before the LORD
your God at Horeb, when he said to me, "Assemble
the people before me to hear my words so that they
may learn to revere me as long as they live in the
land and may teach them to their children."

Deuteronomy 4:9, 10

These commandments that I give you today are to be
upon your hearts. Impress them on your children.
Talk about them when you sit at home and when
you walk along the road, when you lie down and
when you get up. Tie them as symbols on your
hands and bind them on your foreheads. Write them
on the doorframes of your houses and on your gates.

Deuteronomy 6:6-9

Teach them to your children, talking about them

when you sit at home and when you walk along the road, when you lie down and when you get up.

Deuteronomy 11:19

But Sometimes Punishment Is Necessary

Discipline your son, and he will give you peace; he will bring delight to your soul.

Proverbs 29:17

He who spares the rod hates his son, but he who loves him is careful to discipline him.

Proverbs 13:24

Do not withhold discipline from a child; if you punish him with the rod, he will not die.

Proverbs 23:13

Help Children Recognize God's Discipline

My son, do not make light of the Lord's discipline, and do not lose heart when he rebukes you, because the Lord disciplines those he loves, and he punishes everyone he accepts as a son.

Endure hardship as discipline; God is treating you as sons. For what son is not disciplined by his father? If you are not disciplined (and everyone undergoes discipline), then you are illegitimate children and not true sons.

99

Moreover, we have all had human fathers who disciplined us and we respected them for it. How much more should we submit to the Father of our spirits and live! Our fathers disciplined us for a little while as they thought best; but God disciplines us for our good, that we may share in his holiness.

No discipline seems pleasant at the time, but painful. Later on, however, it produces a harvest of righteousness and peace for those who have been trained by it.

Hebrews 12:5b-11

Help Children Learn to Persevere

He who loves pleasure will become poor; whoever loves wine and oil will never be rich.

Proverbs 21:17

But mark this: There will be terrible times in the last days. People will be lovers of themselves, lovers of money, boastful, proud, abusive, disobedient to their parents, ungrateful, unholy, without love, unforgiving, slanderous, without self-control, brutal, not lovers of the good, treacherous, rash, conceited, lovers of pleasure rather than lovers of God.

II Timothy 3:1-4

Anyone who does not carry his cross and follow me cannot be my disciple. Suppose one of you wants to build a tower. Will he not first sit down and estimate the cost to see if he has enough money to complete it? For if he lays the foundation and is not able to finish it, everyone who sees it will ridicule him, saying, "This fellow began to build and was not able to finish."

Or suppose a king is about to go to war against another king. Will he not first sit down and consider whether he is able with ten thousand men to oppose the one coming against him with twenty thousand? If he is not able, he will send a delegation while the other is still a long way off and will ask for terms of peace. In the same way, any of you who does not give up everything he has cannot be my disciple.

Salt is good, but if it loses its saltiness, how can it be made salty again? It is fit neither for the soil nor for the manure pile; it is thrown out. He who has ears to hear, let him hear."

Luke 14:27-35

That is why I am suffering as I am. Yet I am not ashamed, because I know whom I have believed, and am convinced that he is able to guard what I have entrusted to him for that day.

II Timothy 1:12

Help Children Resist Their Temptations

What shall we say, then? Shall we go on sinning so that grace may increase? By no means! We died to sin; how can we live in it any longer? Or don't you know that all of us who were baptized into Christ Jesus were baptized into his death? We were therefore buried with him through baptism into death in order that, just as Christ was raised from the dead through the glory of the Father, we too may live a new life.

If we have been united with him like this in his death, we will certainly also be united with him in his resurrection. For we know that our old self was crucified with him so that the body of sin might be rendered powerless, that we should no longer be slaves to sin— because anyone who has died has been freed from sin. . . .

In the same way, count yourselves dead to sin but alive to God in Christ Jesus. Therefore do not let sin reign in your mortal body so that you obey its evil desires.

Romans 6:1-7, 11, 12

No temptation has seized you except what is common to man. And God is faithful; he will not let you be tempted beyond what you can bear. But when you are tempted, he will also provide a way out so that you can stand up under it.

I Corinthians 10:13

Finally, be strong in the Lord and in his mighty power. Put on the full armor of God so that you can take your stand against the devil's schemes. For our struggle is not against flesh and blood, but against the rulers, against the authorities, against the powers of this dark world and against the spiritual forces of evil in the heavenly realms.

Therefore put on the full armor of God, so that when the day of evil comes, you may be able to stand your ground, and after you have done everything, to stand. Stand firm then, with the belt of truth buckled around your waist, with the breastplate of righteousness in place, and with your feet fitted with the readiness that comes from the gospel of peace.

In addition to all this, take up the shield of faith, with which you can extinguish all the flaming arrows of the evil one. Take the helmet of salvation and the sword of the Spirit, which is the word of God. And pray in the Spirit on all occasions with all kinds of prayers and requests.

With this in mind, be alert and always keep on praying for all the saints.

Ephesians 6:10-18

But the Lord is faithful, and he will strengthen and protect you from the evil one.

II Thessalonians 3:3

Be self-controlled and alert. Your enemy the devil prowls around like a roaring lion looking for someone to devour. Resist him, standing firm in the faith, because you know that your brothers throughout the world are undergoing the same kind of sufferings. And the God of all grace, who called you to his eternal glory in Christ, after you have suffered a little while, will himself restore you and make you strong, firm and steadfast.

I Peter 5:8-10

Help Children Choose God's Will

This day I call heaven and earth as witnesses against you that I have set before you life and death, blessings and curses. Now choose life, so that you and your children may live.

Deuteronomy 30:19

But if serving the LORD seems undesirable to you, then choose for yourselves this day whom you will serve, whether the gods your forefathers served beyond the River, or the gods of the Amorites, in whose land you are living. But as for me and my household, we will serve the LORD."

Joshua 24:15

Help Children Develop Accountability

He who heeds discipline shows the way to life, but whoever ignores correction leads others astray.

Proverbs 10:17

He who scorns instruction will pay for it, but he who respects a command is rewarded.

Proverbs 13:13

The faithless will be fully repaid for their ways, and the good man rewarded for his.

Proverbs 14:14

He who listens to a life-giving rebuke
will be at home among the wise.
He who ignores discipline despises himself,
but whoever heeds correction gains understanding.
The fear of the LORD teaches a man wisdom,
and humility comes before honor.

Proverbs 15:31-33

To the Government

Everyone must submit himself to the governing

105

authorities, for there is no authority except that which God has established. The authorities that exist have been established by God. Consequently, he who rebels against the authority is rebelling against what God has instituted, and those who do so will bring judgment on themselves. For rulers hold no terror for those who do right, but for those who do wrong. Do you want to be free from fear of the one in authority?

Then do what is right and he will commend you. For he is God's servant to do you good. But if you do wrong, be afraid, for he does not bear the sword for nothing. He is God's servant, an agent of wrath to bring punishment on the wrongdoer. Therefore, it is necessary to submit to the authorities, not only because of possible punishment but also because of conscience. This is also why you pay taxes, for the authorities are God's servants, who give their full time to governing. Give everyone what you owe him: If you owe taxes, pay taxes; if revenue, then revenue; if respect, then respect; if honor, then honor. Let no debt remain outstanding, except the continuing debt to love one another, for he who loves his fellowman has fulfilled the law. . . .

Let us behave decently, as in the daytime, not in orgies and drunkenness, not in sexual immorality and debauchery, not in dissension and jealousy. Rather, clothe yourselves with the Lord Jesus Christ, and do not think about how to gratify the desires of the sinful nature.

Romans 13:1-14

In Their Associations

Blessed is the man who does not walk
in the counsel of the wicked
or stand in the way of sinners
or sit in the seat of mockers.
But his delight is in the law of the LORD,
and on his law he meditates day and night.

Psalm 1:1, 2

A righteous man is cautious in friendship, but the way of the wicked leads them astray.

Proverbs 12:26

A perverse man stirs up dissension, and a gossip separates close friends.

Proverbs 16:28

He who loves a pure heart and whose speech is gracious will have the king for his friend.

Proverbs 22:11

Do not make friends with a hot-tempered man, do not associate with one easily angered.

Proverbs 22:24

Wounds from a friend can be trusted, but an enemy multiplies kisses.

Proverbs 27:6

Do not forsake your friend and the friend of your father, and do not go to your brother's house when disaster strikes you—better a neighbor nearby than a brother far away.

Proverbs 27:10

If one falls down, his friend can help him up. But pity the man who falls and has no one to help him up!

Ecclesiastes 4:10

In Their Responsibilities

I went past the field of the sluggard,
past the vineyard of the man who lacks judgment;
thorns had come up everywhere,
the ground was covered with weeds,
and the stone wall was in ruins.
I applied my heart to what I observed
and learned a lesson from what I saw:
A little sleep, a little slumber,
a little folding of the hands to rest—
and poverty will come on you like a bandit
and scarcity like an armed man.

Proverbs 24:30-34

Do you not know that in a race all the runners run, but only one gets the prize? Run in such a way as to get the prize. Everyone who competes in the games goes into strict training. They do it to get a crown that will not last; but we do it to get a crown that will last forever. Therefore I do not run like a man running aimlessly; I do not fight like a man beating the air. No, I beat my body and make it my slave so that after I have preached to others, I myself will not be disqualified for the prize.

I Corinthians 9:24-27

Mind your own business and work with your hands, just as we told you, so that your daily life may win the respect of outsiders and so that you will not be dependent on anybody.

I Thessalonians 4:11b, 12

For even when we were with you, we gave you this rule: "If a man will not work, he shall not eat." We hear that some among you are idle. They are not busy; they are busybodies.

Such people we command and urge in the Lord Jesus Christ to settle down and earn the bread they eat.

II Thessalonians 3:10-12

To Their God

"Not everyone who says to me, 'Lord, Lord,' will enter the kingdom of heaven, but only he who does the will of my Father who is in heaven. Many will say to me on that day, 'Lord, Lord, did we not prophesy in your name, and in your name drive out demons and perform many miracles?'

Then I will tell them plainly, 'I never knew you. Away from me, you evildoers!' "Therefore everyone who hears these words of mine and puts them into practice is like a wise man who built his house on the rock.

The rain came down, the streams rose, and the winds blew and beat against that house; yet it did not fall, because it had its foundation on the rock. But everyone who hears these words of mine and does not put them into practice is like a foolish man who built his house on sand. The rain came down, the streams rose, and the winds blew and beat against that house, and it fell with a great crash." When Jesus had finished saying these things, the crowds were amazed at his teaching.

Matthew 7:21-28

Do not merely listen to the word, and so deceive yourselves. Do what it says. Anyone who listens to the word but does not do what it says is like a man who looks at his face in a mirror and, after looking at himself, goes away and immediately forgets what he looks like.

But the man who looks intently into the perfect law that gives freedom, and continues to do this, not forgetting what he has heard, but doing it—he will be blessed in what he does.

If anyone considers himself religious and yet does not keep a tight rein on his tongue, he deceives himself and his religion is worthless. Religion that God our Father accepts as pure and faultless is this: to look after orphans and widows in their distress and to keep oneself from being polluted by the world.

James 1:22-27

FOR PERSONAL PRAYER:

Lord, when it comes to correcting my children, I've sometimes lost my temper. Occasionally I've viewed my child as a bother or just an interruption to my plans, and I've lashed out. Forgive me, Lord. And give me the strength to start over with a fresh perspective. Amen.

111

CHAPTER 7

'Where do I start when it comes to teaching values?'

"Countless values flow through to us in the Scriptures," declared Jana. "But I think we have to start with the things we feel comfortable modeling in our own lives. We can't give away something we don't have ourselves.

"So I just consider what I'm doing at any given time and think about what kinds of values my actions are displaying in that situation. I look for opportunities to show my kids that I'm aware of what I'm doing, and—most importantly—why I'm doing it."

> **FOR MEMORY:**
> Do not conform any longer to the pattern of this world, but be transformed by the renewing of your mind. Then you will be able to test and approve what God's will is—his good, pleasing and perfect will.
>
> *Romans 12:2*

FOR SILENT REFLECTION:

- *Do I have a clear understanding of how God wants me to live?*

- *What will I do today that shows what I really value in my life?*

- *How will my child know that I care about certain values?*

What Values Are you Modeling?

Since, then, you have been raised with Christ, set your hearts on things above, where Christ is seated at the right hand of God. Set your minds on things above, not on earthly things. For you died, and your life is now hidden with Christ in God. When Christ, who is your life, appears, then you also will appear with him in glory. Put to death, therefore, whatever belongs to your earthly nature: sexual immorality, impurity, lust, evil desires and greed, which is idolatry. Because of these, the wrath of God is coming.

Colossians 3:1-6

Do not love the world or anything in the world. If anyone loves the world, the love of the Father is not in him. For everything in the world—the cravings of sinful man, the lust of his eyes and the boasting of what he has and does—comes not from the Father but from the world. The world and its desires pass away, but the man who does the will of God lives forever.

I John 2:15-17

Therefore, prepare your minds for action; be self-controlled; set your hope fully on the grace to be given you when Jesus Christ is revealed.

I Peter 1:13

Delilah: A Woman of Deceitful Values

Some time later, [Samson] fell in love with a woman in the Valley of Sorek whose name was Delilah. The rulers of the Philistines went to her and said, "See if you can lure him into showing you the secret of his great strength and how we can overpower him so we may tie him up and subdue him. Each one of us will give you eleven hundred shekels of silver." So Delilah said to Samson, "Tell me the secret of your great strength and how you can be tied up and subdued." . . .

Then she said to him, "How can you say, 'I love you,' when you won't confide in me? This is the third time you have made a fool of me and haven't told me the secret of your great strength." With such nagging she prodded him day after day until he was tired to death.

So he told her everything. "No razor has ever been used on my head," he said, "because I have been a Nazirite set apart to God since birth. If my head were shaved, my strength would leave me, and I would become as weak as any other man." When Delilah saw that he had told her everything, she sent word to the rulers of the Philistines, "Come back once more; he has told me everything." So the rulers of the Philistines returned with the silver in their hands.

Judges 16:4-6, 15-18

Sapphira: A Woman Who Valued Money Too Highly

Now a man named Ananias, together with his wife Sapphira, also sold a piece of property. With his wife's full knowledge he kept back part of the money for himself, but brought the rest and put it at the apostles' feet. Then Peter said, "Ananias, how is it that Satan has so filled your heart that you have lied to the Holy Spirit and have kept for yourself some of the money you received for the land? Didn't it belong to you before it was sold? And after it was sold, wasn't the money at your disposal? What made you think of doing such a thing? You have not lied to men but to God."

When Ananias heard this, he fell down and died. And great fear seized all who heard what had happened. Then the young men came forward, wrapped up his body, and carried him out and buried him.

About three hours later his wife came in, not knowing what had happened. Peter asked her, "Tell me, is this the price you and Ananias got for the land?" "Yes," she said, "that is the price." Peter said to her, "How could you agree to test the Spirit of the Lord? Look! The feet of the men who buried your husband are at the door, and they will carry you out also." At that moment she fell down at his feet and died. Then the young men came in and, finding her dead, carried her out and buried her beside her husband.

Acts 5:1-10

Dorcas: A Woman of Good Works

In joppa there was a disciple named Tabitha (which, when translated, is Dorcas), who was always doing good and helping the poor. About that time she became sick and died, and her body was washed and placed in an upstairs room.

Lydda was near Joppa; so when the disciples heard that Peter was in Lydda, they sent two men to him and urged him, "Please come at once!" Peter went with them, and when he arrived he was taken upstairs to the room. All the widows stood around him, crying and showing him the robes and other clothing that Dorcas had made while she was still with them.

Acts 9:36-39

God's Values to Teach Your Children

Perseverance

If a man is lazy, the rafters sag; if his hands are idle, the house leaks.

Ecclesiasted 10:18

Do not be overcome by evil, but overcome evil with good.

Romans 12:21

Jesus looked at them and said, "With man this is

impossible, but with God all things are possible."

Matthew 19:26

He who stands firm to the end will be saved.

Matthew 24:13

Brothers, I do not consider myself yet to have taken hold of it. But one thing I do: Forgetting what is behind and straining toward what is ahead, I press on toward the goal to win the prize for which God has called me heavenward in Christ Jesus.

Philippians 3:13, 14

You then, my son, be strong in the grace that is in Christ Jesus. And the things you have heard me say in the presence of many witnesses entrust to reliable men who will also be qualified to teach others. Endure hardship with us like a good soldier of Christ Jesus.

II Timothy 2:1-3

Then he said to them, "Suppose one of you has a friend, and he goes to him at midnight and says, 'Friend, lend me three loaves of bread, because a friend of mine on a journey has come to me, and I have nothing to set before him.' Then the one inside answers, 'Don't bother me. The door is already locked, and my children are with me in bed. I can't get up and give you anything.' I tell you, though he will not get up and give him the bread because he is his friend, yet because of the man's boldness he will get up and give him as much as he needs.

So I say to you: Ask and it will be given to you; seek and you will find; knock and the door will be opened to you. For everyone who asks receives; he who seeks finds; and to him who knocks, the door will be opened.

Luke 11:5-10

Then Jesus told them this parable: "Suppose one of you has a hundred sheep and loses one of them. Does he not leave the ninety-nine in the open country and go after the lost sheep until he finds it? And when he finds it, he joyfully puts it on his shoulders and goes home.

Then he calls his friends and neighbors together and says, 'Rejoice with me; I have found my lost sheep.' I tell you that in the same way there will be more rejoicing in heaven over one sinner who repents than over ninety-nine righteous persons who do not need to repent.

Or suppose a woman has ten silver coins and loses one. Does she not light a lamp, sweep the house and search carefully until she finds it? And when she finds it, she calls her friends and neighbors together and says, 'Rejoice with me; I have found my lost coin.' In the same way, I tell you, there is rejoicing in the presence of the angels of God over one sinner who repents."

Luke 15:3-10

Thoughtfulness

Do not withhold good from those who deserve it, when it is in your power to act.

Proverbs 3:27

In everything, do to others what you would have them do to you, for this sums up the Law and the Prophets.

Matthew 7:12

The King will reply, "I tell you the truth, whatever you did for one of the least of these brothers of mine, you did for me."

Matthew 25:40

But I tell you who hear me: Love your enemies, do good to those who hate you.

Luke 6:27

Be devoted to one another in brotherly love. Honor one another above yourselves.

Romans 12:10

121

And now these three remain: faith, hope and love.
But the greatest of these is love.

I Corinthians 13:13

Then the servant took ten of his master's camels and left, taking with him all kinds of good things from his master. He set out for Aram Naharaim and made his way to the town of Nahor. He had the camels kneel down near the well outside the town; it was toward evening, the time the women go out to draw water.

Then he prayed, "O LORD, God of my master Abraham, give me success today, and show kindness to my master Abraham. See, I am standing beside this spring, and the daughters of the townspeople are coming out to draw water. May it be that when I say to a girl, 'Please let down your jar that I may have a drink,' and she says, 'Drink, and I'll water your camels too'—let her be the one you have chosen for your servant Isaac. By this I will know that you have shown kindness to my master."

Before he had finished praying, Rebekah came out with her jar on her shoulder. She was the daughter of Bethuel son of Milcah, who was the wife of Abraham's brother Nahor.

The girl was very beautiful, a virgin; no man had ever lain with her. She went down to the spring, filled her jar and came up again. The servant hurried to meet her and said, "Please give me a little water from your jar." "Drink, my lord," she said, and quickly lowered the jar to her hands and gave him a drink. After she had given him a drink, she said, "I'll draw water for your camels too, until they have finished drinking." So she quickly emptied her jar into the trough, ran back to the well to draw more water, and drew enough for all his camels.

Genesis 24:10-20

Six days before the Passover, Jesus arrived at Bethany, where Lazarus lived, whom Jesus had raised from the dead. Here a dinner was given in Jesus' honor. Martha served, while Lazarus was among those reclining at the table with him. Then Mary took about a pint of pure nard, an expensive perfume; she poured it on Jesus' feet and wiped his feet with her hair. And the house was filled with the fragrance of the perfume.

But one of his disciples, Judas Iscariot, who was later to betray him, objected, "Why wasn't this perfume sold and the money given to the poor? It was worth a year's wages." He did not say this because he cared about the poor but because he was a thief; as keeper of the money bag, he used to help himself to what was put into it. "Leave her alone," Jesus replied. "It was intended that she should save this perfume for the day of my burial.

John 12:1-7

Happiness

Boaz took Ruth and she became his wife. Then he went to her, and the LORD enabled her to conceive, and she gave birth to a son. The women said to Naomi: "Praise be to the LORD, who this day has not left you without a kinsman-redeemer. May he become famous throughout Israel! He will renew your life and sustain you in your old age. For your daughter-in-law, who loves you and who is better to you than seven sons, has given him birth." Then Naomi took the child, laid him in her lap and cared for him. The women living there said, "Naomi has a son." And they named him Obed. He was the father of Jesse, the father of David.

Ruth 4:13-17

The LORD has done great things for us, and we are filled with joy.

Psalm 126:3

A happy heart makes the face cheerful, but heartache crushes the spirit.

Proverbs 15:13

A cheerful heart is good medicine, but a crushed spirit dries up the bones.

Proverbs 17:22

124

I know that there is nothing better for men than to be happy and do good while they live.

Ecclesiastes 3:12

They brought them before the magistrates and said, "These men are Jews, and are throwing our city into an uproar by advocating customs unlawful for us Romans to accept or practice." The crowd joined in the attack against Paul and Silas, and the magistrates ordered them to be stripped and beaten. After they had been severely flogged, they were thrown into prison, and the jailer was commanded to guard them carefully. Upon receiving such orders, he put them in the inner cell and fastened their feet in the stocks. About midnight Paul and Silas were praying and singing hymns to God, and the other prisoners were listening to them.

Acts 16:20-25

Honesty

Do not steal. Do not lie. Do not deceive one another.

Leviticus 19:11

If you sell land to one of your countrymen or buy any from him, do not take advantage of each other. You are to buy from your countryman on the basis of the number of years since the Jubilee. And he is to sell to you on the basis of the number of years left for harvesting crops.

When the years are many, you are to increase the price, and when the years are few, you are to decrease the price, because what he is really selling you is the number of crops. Do not take advantage of each other, but fear your God. I am the LORD your God.

Leviticus 25:14-17

You must have accurate and honest weights and measures, so that you may live long in the land the LORD your God is giving you. For the LORD your God detests anyone who does these things, anyone who deals dishonestly.

Deuteronomy 25:15, 16

Keep me from deceitful ways;
be gracious to me through your law.
I have chosen the way of truth;
I have set my heart on your laws.
I hold fast to your statutes, O LORD;
do not let me be put to shame.
I run in the path of your commands,
for you have set my heart free.
Teach me, O LORD, to follow your decrees;
then I will keep them to the end.
Give me understanding,
and I will keep your law and obey it with all my heart.

126

Direct me in the path of your commands,
for there I find delight.
Turn my heart toward your statutes
and not toward selfish gain.
Turn my eyes away from worthless things;
renew my life according to your word.

Psalm 119:29-37

Do not lie to each other, since you have taken off
your old self with its practices and have put on the
new self, which is being renewed in knowledge in
the image of its Creator.

Colossians 3:9, 10

Compassion

On one occasion an expert in the law stood up to
test Jesus. "Teacher," he asked, "what must I do to
inherit eternal life?"

"What is written in the Law?" he replied. "How do
you read it?"

He answered: "'Love the Lord your God with all
your heart and with all your soul and with all your
strength and with all your mind'; and, 'Love your
neighbor as yourself.'" "You have answered cor-
rectly," Jesus replied. "Do this and you will live."

But he wanted to justify himself, so he asked
Jesus, "And who is my neighbor?"

In reply Jesus said: "A man was going down from Jerusalem to Jericho, when he fell into the hands of robbers. They stripped him of his clothes, beat him and went away, leaving him half dead.

A priest happened to be going down the same road, and when he saw the man, he passed by on the other side. So too, a Levite, when he came to the place and saw him, passed by on the other side. But a Samaritan, as he traveled, came where the man was; and when he saw him, he took pity on him. He went to him and bandaged his wounds, pouring on oil and wine.

Then he put the man on his own donkey, took him to an inn and took care of him. The next day he took out two silver coins and gave them to the innkeeper. 'Look after him,' he said, 'and when I return, I will reimburse you for any extra expense you may have.'

"Which of these three do you think was a neighbor to the man who fell into the hands of robbers?"

The expert in the law replied, "The one who had mercy on him."

Jesus told him, "Go and do likewise."

Luke 10:25-37

Faith

Even though I walk through the valley of the shadow of death, I will fear no evil, for you are with me;

your rod and your staff, they comfort me.

Psalm 23: 4

Say to those with fearful hearts, "Be strong, do not fear; your God will come, he will come with vengeance; with divine retribution he will come to save you."

Isaiah 35: 4

I tell you the truth, if you have faith as small as a mustard seed, you can say to this mountain, 'Move from here to there' and it will move. Nothing will be impossible for you."

Matthew 17:20b

For nothing is impossible with God."

Luke 1:37

So I say to you: Ask and it will be given to you; seek and you will find; knock and the door will be opened to you.

Luke 11:9

Without faith it is impossible to please God, because anyone who comes to him must believe that he exists and that he rewards those who earnestly seek him.

-Hebrews 11.6

For everyone born of God overcomes the world. This is the victory that has overcome the world, even our faith. . . . This is the confidence we have in approaching God: that if we ask anything according to his will, he hears us. And if we know that he hears us—whatever we ask—we know that we have what we asked of him.

I John 5:4, 14, 15

FOR PERSONAL PRAYER:

Lord, keep me aware that values are more than just issues to speak about. My values come through loud and clear to my children in the way I live, moment by moment. May you lead me into complete obedience today. Amen.

CHAPTER 8

'How can I handle the pain I feel over the loss of a child?'

I never even imagined that one of my children could be taken away from me like that," said Clair, shortly after the accidental death of her infant son. "Kids aren't supposed to die; that's for old people. But it happened. At first I felt like my whole life would—should—come to an end, too. I really didn't want to go on without him.

"I know that the sense of loss can also be great for mothers who miscarry or when a child runs away from home or walks away from the faith. If you're like me, you can only cling to the promise of God's presence, even when He seems so far away."

131

FOR MEMORY:

Call upon me in the day of trouble; I will deliver you, and you will honor me."

Psalm 50:15

FOR SILENT REFLECTION:

- *Am I harboring any false guilt about what happened?*

- *What forms of bitterness do I need to admit and express? Can I share these feelings with God?*

- *Have I allowed myself to grieve by feeling all the sadness and pain, rather than running from it?*

- *Who in my life can accept my pain without feeling threatened? When did I talk with this person last?*

Facing the Tragedy

Oh, my anguish, my anguish! I writhe in pain. Oh, the agony of my heart! My heart pounds within me, I cannot keep silent.

Jeremiah 4:19a

Why is my pain unending and my wound grievous and incurable? Will you be to me like a deceptive brook, like a spring that fails?

Jeremiah 15:18

He has driven me away and made me walk
in darkness rather than light; indeed,
he has turned his hand against
me again and again, all day long.
He has made my skin and my flesh grow old
and has broken my bones.
He has besieged me and surrounded me
with bitterness and hardship.
He has made me dwell in darkness
like those long dead.
He has walled me in so I cannot escape;
he has weighed me down with chains.
Even when I call out or cry for help,
he shuts out my prayer.
He has barred my way with blocks of stone;
he has made my paths crooked.

133

Like a bear lying in wait, like a lion in hiding,
he dragged me from the path and mangled me
and left me without help.
He drew his bow and made me
the target for his arrows.
He pierced my heart with arrows from his quiver.
I became the laughingstock of all my people;
they mock me in song all day long.
He has filled me with bitter herbs
and sated me with gall.
He has broken my teeth with gravel;
he has trampled me in the dust.
I have been deprived of peace;
I have forgotten what prosperity is.
So I say, "My splendor is gone
and all that I had hoped from the LORD."
I remember my affliction and my wandering,
the bitterness and the gall.
I well remember them,
and my soul is downcast within me.
Yet this I call to mind and therefore I have hope:
Because of the LORD'S great love
we are not consumed,
for his compassions never fail.
They are new every morning;
great is your faithfulness.
I say to myself, "The LORD is my portion;
therefore I will wait for him."

The LORD is good to those whose hope is in him,
to the one who seeks him . . . .
Though he brings grief,
he will show compassion,
so great is his unfailing love.

Lamentations 3:2-25, 32

When I tried to understand all this, it was oppressive
to me.

Psalm 73:16

A Woman Suffering Great Loss

But the king took Armoni and Mephibosheth, the
two sons of Aiah's daughter Rizpah, whom she had
borne to Saul, together with the five sons of Saul's
daughter Merab, whom she had borne to Adriel son
of Barzillai the Meholathite. He handed them over to
the Gibeonites, who killed and exposed them on a
hill before the LORD. All seven of them fell together;
they were put to death during the first days of the
harvest, just as the barley harvest was beginning. Rizpah daughter of Aiah took sackcloth and spread it
out for herself on a rock. From the beginning of the
harvest till the rain poured down from the heavens
on the bodies, she did not let the birds of the air
touch them by day or the wild animals by night.

II Samuel 21:8-10

135

A Mother Grieving in the Wrong Way

Now two prostitutes came to the king and stood before him. One of them said, "My lord, this woman and I live in the same house. I had a baby while she was there with me. The third day after my child was born, this woman also had a baby. We were alone; there was no one in the house but the two of us

"During the night this woman's son died because she lay on him. So she got up in the middle of the night and took my son from my side while I your servant was asleep.

She put him by her breast and put her dead son by my breast. The next morning, I got up to nurse my son—and he was dead! But when I looked at him closely in the morning light, I saw that it wasn't the son I had borne."

The other woman said, "No! The living one is my son; the dead one is yours." But the first one insisted, "No! The dead one is yours; the living one is mine." And so they argued before the king.

The king said, "This one says, 'My son is alive and your son is dead,' while that one says, 'No! Your son is dead and mine is alive.'" Then the king said, "Bring me a sword." So they brought a sword for the king. He then gave an order: "Cut the living child in two and give half to one and half to the other."

The woman whose son was alive was filled with compassion for her son and said to the king, "Please, my lord, give her the living baby! Don't kill him!"

But the other said, "Neither I nor you shall have him. Cut him in two!" Then the king gave his ruling: "Give the living baby to the first woman. Do not kill him; she is his mother."

When all Israel heard the verdict the king had given, they held the king in awe, because they saw that he had wisdom from God to administer justice.

I Kings 3:16-28

Husbands Feeling the Pain, Too

On the seventh day the child died. David's servants were afraid to tell him that the child was dead, for they thought, "While the child was still living, we spoke to David but he would not listen to us. How can we tell him the child is dead? He may do something desperate."

David noticed that his servants were whispering among themselves and he realized the child was dead. "Is the child dead?" he asked. "Yes," they replied, "he is dead." Then David got up from the ground. After he had washed, put on lotions and changed his clothes, he went into the house of the LORD and worshiped.

Then he went to his own house, and at his request they served him food, and he ate. His servants asked him, "Why are you acting this way? While the child was alive, you fasted and wept, but now that the child is dead, you get up and eat!" He answered, "While the child was still alive, I fasted and wept. I thought, 'Who knows? The LORD may be gracious to me and let the child live.' But now that he is dead, why should I fast? Can I bring him back again? I will go to him, but he will not return to me."

II Samuel 12:18-23

One day when Job's sons and daughters were feasting and drinking wine at the oldest brother's house, a messenger came to Job and said, "The oxen were plowing and the donkeys were grazing nearby, and the Sabeans attacked and carried them off. They put the servants to the sword, and I am the only one who has escaped to tell you!"

While he was still speaking, another messenger came and said, "The fire of God fell from the sky and burned up the sheep and the servants, and I am the only one who has escaped to tell you!"

While he was still speaking, another messenger came and said, "The Chaldeans formed three raiding parties and swept down on your camels and carried them off. They put the servants to the sword, and I am the only one who has escaped to tell you!"

While he was still speaking, yet another messenger came and said, "Your sons and daughters were feasting and drinking wine at the oldest brother's house, when suddenly a mighty wind swept in from the desert and struck the four corners of the house. It collapsed on them and they are dead, and I am the only one who has escaped to tell you!"

At this, Job got up and tore his robe and shaved his head. Then he fell to the ground in worship and said: "Naked I came from my mother's womb, and naked I will depart. The LORD gave and the LORD has taken away; may the name of the LORD be praised."

Job 1;13-21

God Comforts Us in Our Loss

He Never Forsakes Us
Call upon me in the day of trouble; I will deliver you, and you will honor me."

Psalm 50:15

Cast your cares on the LORD and he will sustain you; he will never let the righteous fall.

Psalm 55:22

And I will ask the Father, and he will give you another Counselor to be with you forever— the Spirit of truth. The world cannot accept him, because it neither sees him nor knows him. But you know him,

139

for he lives with you and will be in you. I will not leave you as orphans; I will come to you. Before long, the world will not see me anymore, but you will see me. Because I live, you also will live. . . .

Peace I leave with you; my peace I give you. I do not give to you as the world gives. Do not let your hearts be troubled and do not be afraid.

John 14:16-19, 27

But Zion said, "The LORD has forsaken me, the Lord has forgotten me."

"Can a mother forget the baby at her breast and have no compassion on the child she has borne? Though she may forget, I will not forget you!

Isaiah 49:14, 15

Who is a God like you, who pardons sin and forgives the transgression of the remnant of his inheritance? You do not stay angry forever but delight to show mercy. You will again have compassion on us; you will tread our sins underfoot and hurl all our iniquities into the depths of the sea.

Micah 7:18, 19

Therefore, brothers, since we have confidence to enter the Most Holy Place by the blood of Jesus, by a new and living way opened for us through the curtain, that is, his body, and since we have a great priest over the house of God, let us draw near to God with a sincere heart in full assurance of faith, having our hearts sprinkled to cleanse us from a guilty conscience and having our bodies washed with pure water.

Hebrews 10:19-22

In this way, love is made complete among us so that we will have confidence on the day of judgment, because in this world we are like him. There is no fear in love. But perfect love drives out fear, because fear has to do with punishment. The one who fears is not made perfect in love.

I John 4:17, 18

He Provides the Reward of Heaven

Now we know that if the earthly tent we live in is destroyed, we have a building from God, an eternal house in heaven, not built by human hands. Meanwhile we groan, longing to be clothed with our heavenly dwelling, because when we are clothed, we will not be found naked. For while we are in this tent, we groan and are burdened, because we do not wish to be unclothed but to be clothed with our heavenly dwelling, so that what is mortal may be swallowed up by life. Now it is God who has made us for this very purpose and has given us the Spirit as a deposit, guaranteeing what is to come.

Therefore we are always confident and know that as long as we are at home in the body we are away from the Lord.

II Corinthians 5:1-6

Then I saw a new heaven and a new earth, for the first heaven and the first earth had passed away, and there was no longer any sea. I saw the Holy City, the new Jerusalem, coming down out of heaven from God, prepared as a bride beautifully dressed for her husband. And I heard a loud voice from the throne saying, "Now the dwelling of God is with men, and he will live with them. They will be his people, and God himself will be with them and be their God. He will wipe every tear from their eyes. There will be no more death or mourning or crying or pain, for the old order of things has passed away."

Revelation 21:1-4

The city was laid out like a square, as long as it was wide. He measured the city with the rod and found it to be 12,000 stadia in length, and as wide and high as it is long. He measured its wall and it was 144 cubits thick, by man's measurement, which the angel was using. The wall was made of jasper, and the city of pure gold, as pure as glass. The foundations of the city walls were decorated with every kind of precious stone. The first foundation was jasper, the second sapphire, the third chalcedony, the fourth emerald, the fifth sardonyx, the sixth carnelian, the seventh chrysolite, the eighth beryl, the ninth topaz, the tenth chrysoprase, the eleventh jacinth, and the twelfth amethyst. The twelve gates were twelve pearls, each gate made of a single pearl. The great street of the city was of pure gold, like transparent glass.

I did not see a temple in the city, because the Lord God Almighty and the Lamb are its temple. The city does not need the sun or the moon to shine on it, for the glory of God gives it light, and the Lamb is its lamp. The nations will walk by its light, and the kings of the earth will bring their splendor into it. On no day will its gates ever be shut, for there will be no night there. The glory and honor of the nations will be brought into it. Nothing impure will ever enter it, nor will anyone who does what is shameful or deceitful, but only those whose names are written in the Lamb's book of life.

Revelation 21:16-27

He Brings an End to Death and Grief Forever

I know that my Redeemer lives, and that in the end he will stand upon the earth. And after my skin has been destroyed, yet in my flesh I will see God; I myself will see him with my own eyes—I, and not another. How my heart yearns within me!

Job 19:25-27

Even though I walk through
the valley of the shadow of death,
I will fear no evil, for you are with me;
your rod and your staff, they comfort me.
You prepare a table before me
in the presence of my enemies.
You anoint my head with oil; my cup overflows.
Surely goodness and love will
follow me all the days of my life,
and I will dwell in the house of the LORD forever.

Psalm 23:4-6

For you, O LORD, have delivered my soul from death, my eyes from tears, my feet from stumbling.

Psalm 116:8

Do not be amazed at this, for a time is coming when all who are in their graves will hear his voice and come out—those who have done good will rise to live, and those who have done evil will rise to be condemned.

John 5:28, 29

In my Father's house are many rooms; if it were not so, I would have told you. I am going there to prepare a place for you. And if I go and prepare a place for you, I will come back and take you to be with me that you also may be where I am.

John 14:2, 3

144

I consider that our present sufferings are not worth comparing with the glory that will be revealed in us.

Romans 8:18

However, as it is written: "No eye has seen, no ear has heard, no mind has conceived what God has prepared for those who love him."

I Corinthians 2:9

For what I received I passed on to you as of first importance: that Christ died for our sins according to the Scriptures, that he was buried, that he was raised on the third day according to the Scriptures. . . .

But if it is preached that Christ has been raised from the dead, how can some of you say that there is no resurrection of the dead? If there is no resurrection of the dead, then not even Christ has been raised. And if Christ has not been raised, our preaching is useless and so is your faith. More than that, we are then found to be false witnesses about God, for we have testified about God that he raised Christ from the dead. But he did not raise him if in fact the dead are not raised.

For if the dead are not raised, then Christ has not been raised either. And if Christ has not been raised, your faith is futile; you are still in your sins. Then those also who have fallen asleep in Christ are lost. If only for this life we have hope in Christ, we are to be pitied more than all men. But Christ has indeed been raised from the dead, the firstfruits of those who have fallen asleep. . . .

Listen, I tell you a mystery: We will not all sleep, but we will all be changed— in a flash, in the twinkling of an eye, at the last trumpet. For the trumpet will sound, the dead will be raised imperishable, and we will be changed. For the perishable must clothe itself with the imperishable, and the mortal with immortality. When the perishable has been clothed with the imperishable, and the mortal with immortality, then the saying that is written will come true: "Death has been swallowed up in victory."

"Where, O death, is your victory? Where, O death, is your sting?"

I Corinthians 15:3-54

Brothers, we do not want you to be ignorant about those who fall asleep, or to grieve like the rest of men, who have no hope. We believe that Jesus died and rose again and so we believe that God will bring with Jesus those who have fallen asleep in him. According to the Lord's own word, we tell you that we who are still alive, who are left till the coming of the Lord, will certainly not precede those who have fallen asleep. For the Lord himself will come down from heaven, with a loud command, with the voice of the archangel and with the trumpet call of God, and the dead in Christ will rise first. After that, we who are still alive and are left will be caught up together with them in the clouds to meet the Lord in the air. And so we will be with the Lord forever. Therefore encourage each other with these words.

I Thessalonians 4:13-18

But in keeping with his promise we are looking forward to a new heaven and a new earth, the home of righteousness.

II Peter 3:13

After this I looked and there before me was a great multitude that no one could count, from every nation, tribe, people and language, standing before the throne and in front of the Lamb. They were wearing white robes and were holding palm branches in their hands. And they cried out in a loud voice: "Salvation belongs to our God, who sits on the throne, and to the Lamb." All the angels were standing around the throne and around the elders and the four living creatures. They fell down on their faces before the throne and worshiped God, saying: "Amen! Praise and glory and wisdom and thanks and honor and power and strength be to our God for ever and ever. Amen!"

Then one of the elders asked me, "These in white robes who are they, and where did they come from?" I answered, "Sir, you know." And he said, "These are they who have come out of the great tribulation; they have washed their robes and made them white in the blood of the Lamb. Therefore, "they are before the throne of God and serve him day and night in his temple; and he who sits on the throne will spread his tent over them. Never again will they hunger; never again will they thirst. The sun will not beat upon them, nor any scorching heat. For the Lamb at the center of the throne will be their shepherd; he will lead them to springs of living water. And God will wipe away every tear from their eyes."

Revelation 7:9-17

FOR PERSONAL PRAYER:

Lord, I do not ask You to make me understand why this happened. I only ask that you bring Your comfort into my life to soothe my pain. I need to know that You are close. I am so thankful that You never leave me, even in my most bitter and angry moments. Amen.

CHAPTER 9

'What should I teach my kids about God?'

I t's amazing what kids—even very little kids—can understand about God," said Rhonda. They can certainly understand love and care by everything we, as moms, do to nurture them at home. When they get a little older they can start learning some pretty deep theological concepts, too.

"But I don't want my kids just to know *about* God; I want them to know God in a personal relationship, too. That's why I stress Jesus as the revelation of God in the flesh. We can know what God is truly like because we can see how Jesus lived here on earth. My kids love stories about Jesus."

FOR MEMORY:

For in Christ all the fullness of the Deity lives in bodily form.

Colossians 2:9

FOR SILENT REFLECTION:

- *How much do I know about God's attributes?*

- *What have I taught my children about God recently?*

- *How much of my teaching about God can I convey with examples from my own experience with God?*

- *How well do my kids know who Jesus is?*

Helping Your Kids Know the Awesome God

He Is All-Powerful

Yours, O LORD, is the greatness and the power and the glory and the majesty and the splendor, for everything in heaven and earth is yours. Yours, O LORD, is the kingdom; you are exalted as head over all. Wealth and honor come from you; you are the ruler of all things. In your hands are strength and power to exalt and give strength to all.

I Chronicles 29:11, 12

The LORD is my strength and my shield;
my heart trusts in him, and I am helped.
My heart leaps for joy
and I will give thanks to him in song.
The LORD is the strength of his people,
a fortress of salvation for his anointed one.

Psalm 28:7, 8

The LORD is slow to anger and great in power;
the LORD will not leave the guilty unpunished.
His way is in the whirlwind and the storm,
and clouds are the dust of his feet.
He rebukes the sea and dries it up;
he makes all the rivers run dry.
Bashan and Carmel wither
and the blossoms of Lebanon fade.

151

The mountains quake before him
and the hills melt away.
The earth trembles at his presence,
the world and all who live in it.
Who can withstand his indignation?
Who can endure his fierce anger?
His wrath is poured out like fire;
the rocks are shattered before him.

Nahum 1:3-6

He stood, and shook the earth;
he looked, and made the nations tremble.
The ancient mountains crumbled
and the age-old hills collapsed.
His ways are eternal.
I saw the tents of Cushan in distress,
the dwellings of Midian in anguish.
Were you angry with the rivers, O LORD?
Was your wrath against the streams?
Did you rage against the sea when you rode
with your horses and your victorious chariots?
You uncovered your bow,
you called for many arrows.
You split the earth with rivers;
the mountains saw you and writhed.
Torrents of water swept by;
the deep roared and lifted its waves on high.
Sun and moon stood still in the heavens

at the glint of your flying arrows,
at the lightning of your flashing spear.
In wrath you strode through the earth
and in anger you threshed the nations.
You came out to deliver your people,
to save your anointed one.
You crushed the leader of the land of wickedness,
you stripped him from head to foot.
With his own spear you pierced his head
when his warriors stormed out to scatter us,
gloating as though about to devour
the wretched who were in hiding.
You trampled the sea with your horses,
churning the great waters.

Habakkuk 3:6-15

What, then, shall we say in response to this? If God
is for us, who can be against us?

Romans 8:31

He Is All-Knowing and Wise
By his knowledge the deeps were divided, and the
clouds let drop the dew.

Proverbs 3:20

The LORD brought me, [Wisdom],
forth as the first of his works,
before his deeds of old;

I was appointed from eternity,
from the beginning,
before the world began.
When there were no oceans,
I was given birth, when there were no springs
abounding with water;
before the mountains were settled in place,
before the hills, I was given birth,
before he made the earth
or its fields or any of the dust of the world.
I was there when he set the heavens in place,
when he marked out the horizon on the face of the
deep,
when he established the clouds above
and fixed securely the fountains of the deep,
when he gave the sea its boundary
so the waters would not overstep his command,
and when he marked out the foundations of the
earth.
Then I was the craftsman at his side.
I was filled with delight day after day,
rejoicing always in his presence,
rejoicing in his whole world
and delighting in mankind.

Proverbs 8:22-31

And even the very hairs of your head are all numbered.

Matthew 10:30

He Is Patient
The LORD, the LORD, the compassionate and gracious God, slow to anger, abounding in love and faithfulness.

Exodus 34:6b

The LORD is slow to anger, abounding in love and forgiving sin and rebellion. Yet he does not leave the guilty unpunished; he punishes the children for the sin of the fathers to the third and fourth generation.

Numbers 14:18

Rend your heart and not your garments. Return to the LORD your God, for he is gracious and compassionate, slow to anger and abounding in love, and he relents from sending calamity.

Joel 2:13

How long, O LORD, must I call for help,
but you do not listen?
Or cry out to you, "Violence!"
but you do not save?
Why do you make me look at injustice?
Why do you tolerate wrong?

Destruction and violence are before me;
there is strife, and conflict abounds.
Therefore the law is paralyzed,
and justice never prevails.
The wicked hem in the righteous,
so that justice is perverted.

Habakkuk 1:2-4

Or do you show contempt for the riches of his kindness, tolerance and patience, not realizing that God's
kindness leads you toward repentance?

Romans 2:4

May the God who gives endurance and encourage-
ment give you a spirit of unity among yourselves as
you follow Christ Jesus.

Romans 15:5

He Is Merciful

For God does speak—now one way,
now another—though man may not perceive it.
In a dream, in a vision of the night,
when deep sleep falls on men
as they slumber in their beds,
he may speak in their ears and terrify them with
warnings,
to turn man from wrongdoing
and keep him from pride,

to preserve his soul from the pit,
his life from perishing by the sword. . . .
He prays to God and finds favor with him,
he sees God's face and shouts for joy;
he is restored by God to his righteous state.
Then he comes to men and says,
"I sinned, and perverted what was right,
but I did not get what I deserved.
He redeemed my soul from going down to the pit,
and I will live to enjoy the light."
God does all these things to a man—
twice, even three times—
to turn back his soul from the pit,
that the light of life may shine on him.

Job 33:14-30

Whom have you so dreaded and feared that you
have been false to me, and have neither remembered
me nor pondered this in your hearts? Is it not
because I have long been silent that you do not fear
me?

Isaiah 57:11

For this is what the high and lofty One says—
he who lives forever, whose name is holy:
"I live in a high and holy place,
but also with him who is contrite and lowly in spirit,
to revive the spirit of the lowly

and to revive the heart of the contrite.
I will not accuse forever,
nor will I always be angry,
for then the spirit of man would grow faint before me—
the breath of man that I have created.
I was enraged by his sinful greed;
I punished him, and hid my face in anger,
yet he kept on in his willful ways.
I have seen his ways, but I will heal him;
I will guide him and restore comfort to him,
creating praise on the lips of the mourners in Israel.
Peace, peace, to those far and near," says the LORD.
"And I will heal them."

Isaiah 57:15-19

Be merciful, just as your Father is merciful.

Luke 6:36

For there is no difference between Jew and Gentile—
the same Lord is Lord of all and richly blesses all who call on him.

Romans 10:12

He Is Faithful

Whenever the rainbow appears in the clouds, I will see it and remember the everlasting covenant between God and all living creatures of every kind on the earth.

Genesis 9:16

But it was because the LORD loved you and kept the oath he swore to your forefathers that he brought you out with a mighty hand and redeemed you from the land of slavery, from the power of Pharaoh king of Egypt. Know therefore that the LORD your God is God; he is the faithful God, keeping his covenant of love to a thousand generations of those who love him and keep his commands.

Deuteronomy 7:8, 9

Lift up your eyes to the heavens,
look at the earth beneath;
the heavens will vanish like smoke,
the earth will wear out like a garment
and its inhabitants die like flies.
But my salvation will last forever,
my righteousness will never fail. . . .
For the moth will eat them up like a garment;
the worm will devour them like wool.
But my righteousness will last forever,
my salvation through all generations.

Isaiah 51:6, 8

"To me this is like the days of Noah,
when I swore that the waters of Noah

would never again cover the earth.
So now I have sworn not to be angry with you,
never to rebuke you again.
Though the mountains be shaken
and the hills be removed,
yet my unfailing love for you
will not be shaken nor my covenant
of peace be removed," says the LORD,
who has compassion on you.

Isaiah 54:9, 10

God is not unjust; he will not forget your work and the love you have shown him as you have helped his people and continue to help them. . . . When God made his promise to Abraham, since there was no one greater for him to swear by, he swore by himself, saying, "I will surely bless you and give you many descendants."

And so after waiting patiently, Abraham received what was promised. Men swear by someone greater than themselves, and the oath confirms what is said and puts an end to all argument. Because God wanted to make the unchanging nature of his purpose very clear to the heirs of what was promised, he confirmed it with an oath. God did this so that, by two unchangeable things in which it is impossible for God to lie, we who have fled to take hold of the hope offered to us may be greatly encouraged. We have this hope as an anchor for the soul, firm and secure. It enters the inner sanctuary behind the curtain.

Hebrews 6:10-19

So then, those who suffer according to God's will should commit themselves to their faithful Creator and continue to do good.

I Peter 4:19

He Seeks Faithful Worshipers

Now faith is being sure of what we hope for and certain of what we do not see. This is what the ancients were commended for. By faith we understand that the universe was formed at God's command, so that what is seen was not made out of what was visible. By faith Abel offered God a better sacrifice than Cain did. By faith he was commended as a righteous man, when God spoke well of his offerings. And by faith he still speaks, even though he is dead. By faith Enoch was taken from this life, so that he did not experience death; he could not be found, because God had taken him away. For before he was taken, he was commended as one who pleased God. And without faith it is impossible to please God, because anyone who comes to him must believe that he exists and that he rewards those who earnestly seek him.

Hebrews 11:1-6

Teaching Your Kids Who Jesus Is

He Was God Incarnate

But you, Bethlehem Ephrathah, though you are small among the clans of Judah, out of you will come for me one who will be ruler over Israel, whose origins are from of old, from ancient times.

Micah 5:2

In the beginning was the Word, and the Word was with God, and the Word was God. . . .

The Word became flesh and made his dwelling among us. We have seen his glory, the glory of the One and Only, who came from the Father, full of grace and truth.

John 1:1, 14

Coming to his hometown, he began teaching the people in their synagogue, and they were amazed. "Where did this man get this wisdom and these miraculous powers?" they asked.

Matthew 13:54

Then Jesus came to them and said, "All authority in heaven and on earth has been given to me.

Matthew 28:18

Jesus said to them, "My Father is always at his work

162

to this very day, and I, too, am working." For this reason the Jews tried all the harder to kill him; not only was he breaking the Sabbath, but he was even calling God his own Father, making himself equal with God.

John 5:17, 18

Who, being in very nature God, did not consider equality with God something to be grasped.

Philippians 2:6

Beyond all question, the mystery of godliness is great: He appeared in a body, was vindicated by the Spirit, was seen by angels, was preached among the nations, was believed on in the world, was taken up in glory.

I Timothy 3:16

It is because of him that you are in Christ Jesus, who has become for us wisdom from God—that is, our righteousness, holiness and redemption.

I Corinthians 1:30

He Claimed to Be Deity

"Are you the one who was to come, or should we expect someone else?" Jesus replied, "Go back and report to John what you hear and see: The blind

163

receive sight, the lame walk, those who have leprosy
are cured, the deaf hear, the dead are raised, and the
good news is preached to the poor. Blessed is the
man who does not fall away on account of me."

Matthew 11:3-6

But Jesus remained silent. The high priest said to
him, "I charge you under oath by the living God: Tell
us if you are the Christ, the Son of God." "Yes, it is
as you say," Jesus replied. "But I say to all of you: In
the future you will see the Son of Man sitting at the
right hand of the Mighty One and coming on the
clouds of heaven." Then the high priest tore his
clothes and said, "He has spoken blasphemy! Why
do we need any more witnesses? Look, now you
have heard the blasphemy.

Matthew 26:63-65

He said to them, "How foolish you are, and how
slow of heart to believe all that the prophets have
spoken! Did not the Christ have to suffer these things
and then enter his glory?" And beginning with Moses
and all the Prophets, he explained to them what was
said in all the Scriptures concerning himself.

Luke 24:25-27

The woman said, "I know that Messiah" (called
Christ) "is coming. When he comes, he will explain

everything to us." Then Jesus declared, "I who speak to you am he."

John 4:25, 26

If you believed Moses, you would believe me, for he wrote about me. But since you do not believe what he wrote, how are you going to believe what I say?"

John 5:46, 47

Can any of you prove me guilty of sin? If I am telling the truth, why don't you believe me?

John 8:46

The Jews gathered around him, saying, "How long will you keep us in suspense? If you are the Christ, tell us plainly." Jesus answered, "I did tell you, but you do not believe. The miracles I do in my Father's name speak for me, but you do not believe because you are not my sheep. My sheep listen to my voice; I know them, and they follow me. I give them eternal life, and they shall never perish; no one can snatch them out of my hand. My Father, who has given them to me, is greater than all; no one can snatch them out of my Father's hand. I and the Father are one."

John 10:24-30

Then Jesus cried out, "When a man believes in me, he does not believe in me only, but in the one who sent me. When he looks at me, he sees the one who sent me.

John 12:44, 45

If you really knew me, you would know my Father as well. From now on, you do know him and have seen him." Philip said, "Lord, show us the Father and that will be enough for us." Jesus answered: "Don't you know me, Philip, even after I have been among you such a long time? Anyone who has seen me has seen the Father. How can you say, 'Show us the Father'? Don't you believe that I am in the Father, and that the Father is in me? The words I say to you are not just my own. Rather, it is the Father, living in me, who is doing his work.

John 14:7-10

He Bore Our Sins

Since the children have flesh and blood, he too shared in their humanity so that by his death he might destroy him who holds the power of death— that is, the devil— and free those who all their lives were held in slavery by their fear of death. For surely it is not angels he helps, but Abraham's descendants. For this reason he had to be made like his brothers in every way, in order that he might become a merciful and faithful high priest in service to God, and that he might make atonement for the sins of the people.

Because he himself suffered when he was tempted, he is able to help those who are being tempted.

Hebrews 2:14-18

Therefore I will give him a portion among the great, and he will divide the spoils with the strong, because he poured out his life unto death and was numbered with the transgressors. For he bore the sin of many, and made intercession for the transgressors.

Isaiah 53:12

God made him who had no sin to be sin for us, so that in him we might become the righteousness of God.

II Corinthians 5:21

He himself bore our sins in his body on the tree, so that we might die to sins and live for righteousness; by his wounds you have been healed. For you were like sheep going astray, but now you have returned to the Shepherd and Overseer of your souls.

1 Peter 2:24, 25

Therefore, brothers, since we have confidence to enter the Most Holy Place by the blood of Jesus, by a new and living way opened for us through the curtain, that is, his body, and since we have a great

167

priest over the house of God, let us draw near to God with a sincere heart in full assurance of faith, having our hearts sprinkled to cleanse us from a guilty conscience and having our bodies washed with pure water.

Hebrews 10:19-22

FOR PERSONAL PRAYER:

Lord, open my eyes to the way You teach me about Yourself in daily circumstances. And keep me open to ways I can teach my children about You by the way I model my trust in Your goodness and guidance today. Amen.

BIBLE WISDOM FOR SINGLE PARENTS

'How can I cope with this feeling of being so forsaken?'

'How can I keep my focus on God's goodness rather than on my problems?'

'How can I handle the stress of this balancing act?'

Discover what the Bible has to say in response to these and other important questions in *Bible Wisdom for Single Parents*.

BIBLE WISDOM FOR FATHERS

'What if I never had a good, loving father of my own for a role model?'

'How can I build my home on a solid foundation of spiritual truth?'

'How can I handle my frustrations with this incredible parenting challenge?'

Help in finding Biblical answers to these and other questions commonly voiced by dads everywhere can be found in *Bible Wisdom For Fathers*.

BIBLE WISDOM FOR PARENTS

'What can I do about a home environment that falls far short of "heaven on earth"?'

'What are the lasting values to give my children?'

'What do I do when I feel frustrated with my parenting responsibilities?'

Bible Wisdom for Parents offers help in answering these and other critical questions parents ask.